D0663723

LATIN FOR ALL OCCASIONS

LATIN FOR ALL OCCASIONS

OCCASIONS

(LINGUA LATINA OCCASIONIBUS OMNIBUS)

Newly Revised and Updated Papyrus-back Edition

*Become the Life of the Party with
Everyone's Favorite Dead Language!*

BY HENRY BEARD

Henricus Barbatus Scripsit

Latin Language Advisor
J. MARK SUGARS, PhD

Illustrator
MIKHAIL IVENITSKY

GOTHAM
BOOKS

GOTHAM BOOKS
Published by Penguin Group (USA) Inc.
375 Hudson Street, New York, New York 10014, U.S.A.
Penguin Group (Canada), 10 Alcorn Avenue, Toronto, Ontario, Canada M4V 3B2 (a division of Pearson Penguin Canada Inc.); Penguin Books Ltd, 80 Strand, London WC2R 0RL, England; Penguin Ireland, 25 St Stephen's Green, Dublin 2, Ireland (a division of Penguin Books Ltd.); Penguin Group (Australia), 250 Camberwell Road, Camberwell, Victoria 3124, Australia (a division of Pearson Australia Group Pty Ltd); Penguin Books India Pvt Ltd, 11 Community Centre, Panchsheel Park, New Delhi–110 017, India; Penguin Group (NZ), Cnr Airborne and Rosedale Roads, Albany, Auckland, New Zealand (a division of Pearson New Zealand Ltd); Penguin Books (South Africa) (Pty) Ltd, 24 Sturdee Avenue, Rosebank, Johannesburg 2196, South Africa
Penguin Books Ltd, Registered Offices: 80 Strand, London WC2R 0RL, England

Published by Gotham Books, a division of Penguin Group (USA) Inc.

First American printing, September 2004
10   9   8

Parts of this text were originally published as *Latin for All Occasions* (Villard Books, 1990) and *Latin for Even More Occasions* (Villard Books, 1991)

Gotham Books and the skyscraper logo are trademarks of Penguin Group (USA) Inc.

LIBRARY OF CONGRESS CATALOGING-IN-PUBLICATION DATA
has been applied for.

ISBN: 1-592-40080-9

Printed in the United States of America
Set in Dante MT
Designed by Sabrina Bowers

CONTENTS
INDEX CAPITUM

Preface *(Prefatio)*   vii

    I. Conversational Latin *(Lingua Latina Conlocutioni)*   1

    II. Informational Latin *(Lingua Latina Nuntiis)*   7

    III. Occupational Latin *(Lingua Latina Occupationi)*   15

    IV. Recreational Latin *(Lingua Latina Oblectamentis)*   23

    V. Practical Latin *(Lingua Latina Utilis)*   33

    VI. Tactical Latin *(Lingua Latina Rationi)*   41

    VII. Cultural Latin *(Lingua Latina Docta)*   51

    VIII. Social Latin *(Lingua Latina Vitae Communi)*   59

    IX. Sensual Latin *(Lingua Latina Libidinosa)*   69

    X. Gastronomical Latin *(Lingua Latina Cenatica)*   75

    XI. Familial Latin *(Lingua Latina Domestica)*   83

    XII. Formal Latin *(Lingua Latina Ritibus)*   91

    XIII. Casual Latin *(Lingua Latina Quotidiana)*   97

    XIV. Personal Latin *(Lingua Latina Propria)*   105

    XV. Convivial Latin *(Lingua Latina Hilaris)*   113

    XVI. International Latin *(Lingua Latina Foris)*   121

    XVII. Essential Latin *(Lingua Latina Necessaria)*   129

    XVIII. Pop-Cultural Latin *(Lingua Latina Popularis)*   141

    XIX. Celebrational Latin *(Lingua Latina Festiva)*   153

    XX. A Brief Guide to Latin Pronunciation
         (Locutio Linguae Latinae Paucis Verbis Explanatur)   163

PREFACE
PREFATIO

You know the feeling all too well. There you are, chatting with business associates at an upscale watering hole, or participating in a little good-natured give-and-take during a golf or tennis match, or relaxing with friends on the beach, or maybe just reviewing the day with your family at the supper table. You spot an opportunity to liven up the discussion with a particularly pithy observation in Latin, and then, all of a sudden, you're assailed by paralyzing doubts.

Does the verb you were planning to use belong in the second or third conjugation? Is it irregular? Deponent? Reflexive? Defective? Does it take *ut* and a subjunctive or an infinitive with the accusative? Or, worse still, does it take the dative, or the genitive? Would a gerundive construction be more appropriate, or laughably awkward? How about a passive periphrastic or—but no, it's too late. The moment has passed; the conversation has moved on.

Now, be honest—how many times has that happened to you? If your answer is *saepius* (all too often)—and we bet it is!—then *Lingua Latina Occasionibus Omnibus (Latin for All Occasions)* is the book for you.

Here, in one handy, easy-to-use, toga-totable papyrus-back book, are hundreds of everyday English expressions rendered into grammatically accurate, idiomatically correct classical Latin, just as you would have translated them yourself if you had the time. And all of these practical phrases are conveniently organized into familiar conversational categories so you can be confident that in any social situation some suitable Latin *bona dicta* (*bon mots*) will be right at your fingertips, just as they would be if only you could get in a little more practice.

The next time you feel like using the immortal language of Caesar and Cicero to turn an ordinary remark into a timeless utterance, don't let *feles* (the cat) get your tongue. With a copy of this handy little volume tucked in your sleeve (or in the bag carried by the faithful retainer walking a respectful two paces behind you), you'll never again be intimidated by those seven hundred verb endings, ninety noun cases, and twenty kinds of ablative. And you'll quickly discover that whether you want to impress the boss, entertain your friends, keep the kids in line, or charm that special someone, speaking Latin is as easy as taking Gaul from the Gauls.

Vince! (Knock 'em dead!)

I.
CONVERSATIONAL LATIN
Lingua Latina Conlocutioni

COCKTAIL PARTY CHITCHAT

Hot enough for you?
Satine caloris tibi dies est?

Run into much traffic on the way over?
Eratne turba magna vehiculorum obviam tibi venienti huc?

What do you think I paid for this watch?
Quanto putas mihi stetisse hoc horologium carpale?

You know what I think? I think . . .
Visne scire quid credem? Credo . . .

    that all wrestling is fixed.
    luctationes omnes praestitutas esse.

    that flying saucers are real.
    astronaves orbiculares exsistere.

    that Elvis is still alive.
    Elvem ipsum etiam vivere.

    that the weather has been altered by rocket launches.
    missiones pyraulorum statum caeli mutavisse.

    that no one's barbecue sauce is better than mine.
    neminem facere liquamen assatorium melius quam meum.

CONVERSATION FILLERS

Is that so?
Ain tu?

Really?
Vero?

You don't say!
Dic! Itane est?

You can say that again!
Hercle qui tu recte dicis!

You know what they say . . .
Ut proverbium loquitur vetus . . .

    here today, gone tomorrow.
    quod adest hodie, cras aberit.

    seen one, seen them all.
    uno cum noris, omnia noris.

    what goes around, comes around.
    circumit ad idem, unde profectum est, reveniet.

    que sera, sera.
    quod fiet, fiet.

CONVERSATION ENDERS

God! Look at the time! My wife will kill me!
Di! Ecce hora! Uxor mea me necabit!

Excuse me. I've got to see a man about a dog.
Mihi ignosce. Nunc est mihi cum quodam negotium de cane.

Darn! There goes my beeper!
Heu! Tintinnuntius meus sonat!

I'm outta here.
Abeo.

Have a nice day.
Sit hic dies tibi iucundus.

PITHY LATIN EXPRESSIONS

By that very fact.
Ipso facto.

No way.
Nullo modo.

Read my lips.
Lege labia.

A done deal.
Pactum factum.

Fat chance.
Forsitan fiat.

Accidentally on purpose.
Casu consulto.

Royally screwed.
Raptus regaliter.

In a world of hurt.
Oppido dolens.

Hopefully.
Spes est.

II.
INFORMATIONAL LATIN
Lingua Latina Nuntiis

LATIN SIGNS FOR OUR TIMES

CAVE CANEM
Beware of dog

NOLI PERTURBARE
Do not disturb

NOLI INTRARE
Keep out

OPORTET MINISTROS MANUS LAVARE ANTEQUAM LATRINAM RELINQUANT
Employees must wash hands before leaving restroom

BARBARII IN HOC CURRU NON EST RADIOPHONIUMI
No radio!

TIBI GRATIAS AGIMUS QUOD NIHIL FUMAS
Thank you for not smoking

*SI HOC SIGNUM LEGERE POTES, OPUS REMUNERATIVUM OBTINERE POTES IN
FORO ALACRI LUCRATIVOQUE LINGUAE LATINAE*
If you can read this sign, you can get a good job in the fast-
paced, high-paying world of Latin!

LATIN BUMPER STICKERS FOR YOUR CHARIOT

CURSUM PRO FERIS REFRENO
I brake for animals

CONSERVEMUS BALAENAS
Save the whales

SONA SI LATINE LOQUERIS
Honk if you speak Latin

CUM CATAPULTAE PROSCRIPTAE ERUNT TUM SOLI PROSCRIPTI CATAPULTAS
HABEBUNT
When catapults are outlawed, only outlaws will have
catapults

SI HUNC TITULUM CURRULEM LEGERE POTES, ET LIBERALITER EDUCATUS ES ET
NIMIUM PROPRE ME SEQUERIS
If you can read this bumper sticker, you are both very well
educated and much too close

LICENSE PLATES

INCITATUS
Speed demon

VAGANS
Cruising

LITORALIS
Beach bum

MANNUS
Mustang

FRACTUM
Jalopy

NITIDUS
Snazzy

URSUS
Bear

AMO VI-UM
I love sex

TURBO
Turbo

HACKER LATIN: THE USER-FRIENDLY LANGUAGE

Why won't you print out?
Cur nihil imprimis?

Don't you dare erase my hard disk!
Ne eraseris discum rigidum!

I did not commit a fatal error!
Nullo modo erravi letaliter!

Garbage in, garbage out.
Infuso purgamento, purgamentum exit.

How's hacking, chiphead?
Quid agis, caput assulae?

My motherboard fried! I'm in a pessimal mode!
Tabula materna combusta est! Sum in modo pessimo!

Some bagbiting technoweenie put a hungus Trojan horse in
my program! It is munged!

*Nescioquis coleivorus in meum programma posuit. Pessum datum
est!*

I am globally torqued! Moby bogosity!

Funditus tortus sum! Fucatissimum!

LATIN SPAM—IT'S UNBLOCKABLE!

*Salve, o alienigena! Est mihi nomen Midas. Rex sum Phrygiae,
terrae clarae quae in Asia Minore est. Propter casum infelicem,
omnia quae tango mutantur in aurum. Cuius multa milia
librarum mihi sunt hoc autem quasi vexatium onus deponere
pervolo! Ergo transmitte mihi, sis, numerum rationis tuae in
argentaria taberna, et numeros chartularum fidei tuarum, et
numerum chartulae largitionis senioribus publicae, et nomen avi
tui materni. Numeris receptis, ilico tibi remittam navem
onustam lateribus aureis. Mihi gratum facies manus meas
exonerans his rebus! Tibi multas gratias ago!*

Greetings foreign person! My name is Midas, and I am King
of Phrygia. Owing to an unfortunate accident, everything
I touch turns to gold. I have tons and tons of the stuff—
I'm dying to get rid of the darn stuff! Please send me your
bank account number, your credit card information, your
social security number, and your mother's maiden name,
and I will immediately dispatch to you a boatload of gold
bricks. You'll be doing me a big favor by taking it off my
hands! I am much thanking you!

*XXXXXX! Nuntium bonum de terra prisca litterarum chiasticarum
supervacanearum viris quorum inguinales siphunculi pusilluli
sint! Nunc, per unguenta potentia e sepulcro Pompeiano diu
occulto effosa, potes uti arcanis orgiorum Bacchanalium ad mire
amplificandum machimentum amoris tuum! Elige
magnitudinem membri virilis exoptatum:*

- ❑ *milliarium*
- ❑ *columna Dorica*
- ❑ *Pharus*
- ❑ *Herculis Columna*

XXXXXX! Good news from the original land of too many X's
for men with needle-sized trouser-spouts! Now thanks to
powerful ointments discovered in a long-lost tomb in
Pompeii you can use the ancient secrets of the Bacchanalian
orgies to dramatically enlarge your engine of love! Select
desired dimension of sexual organ:

- ❑ milepost
- ❑ Doric column
- ❑ lighthouse
- ❑ pillar of Hercules

HANDY ACRONYMS FROM THE LAND OF SPQR

Kiss	Keep It Simple, Stupid
SSS	*Sit Simplex, Stulte*
CYA	Cover Your Ass
PTN	*Protege Tuas Nates*
NIMBY	Not in My Backyard
NPIMV	*Ne Ponatur In Mea Vicinitate*

| MEGO | My Eyes Glaze Over |
| OMFL | *Oculi Mei Fiunt Languidi* |

AN ALL-PURPOSE HOLD-UP NOTE

I have a catapult. Give me all the money, or I will fling an
  enormous rock at your head.

Catapultem habeo. Nisi pecuniam omnem mihi dabis, ad caput
  tuum saxum immane mittam.

III.
OCCUPATIONAL LATIN
Lingua Latina Occupationi

NEGOTIATING IN LATIN

I'd like to cut a deal.
Volo pactionem facere.

Now, this isn't carved in stone.
Hoc vero in marmore non est incisum.

This is just a ballpark figure.
Hic est numerus, plus aut minus.

I'm thinking out loud.
Clara voce cogito.

This is all blue sky.
Totum de caelo caeruleo venit.

I think we're on the same wavelength.
Credo nos in fluctu emittere undas radiophonicas eadem frequentia.

SWEETENING THE DEAL

Can you put more money on the table?
Potesne plus pecuniae in mensa ponere?

Let's look at the bottom line.
Summam scrutemur.

Is that your best offer?
Num ista licitatio maxima est?

Can't you sharpen up your pencil a little on this?
Nonne potes stilum tuum in hac re paulum acuere?

If you can't go any higher, the deal is off.
Si plus offerre non possis, pactio retrahetur.

PLAYING HARDBALL

We're back to square one.
In carceribus denuo adsumus.

I'm wasting my time.
Tempus nequiquam tero.

That's the deal. Take it or leave it.
Ecce pactum. Aut accipe aut relinque.

You're not the only game in town.
In hoc oppido lusor unicus non es.

Well, you win some, you lose some.
Modo vincimus, modo vincimur.

HIDDEN INSULTS

Latin	What you say it means	What it really means
Podex perfectus es.	You did a terrific job.	You are a total asshole.
Tu quidem de planeta Martis vere venisti.	That's a truly remarkable thought.	You are clearly from Mars.
Stercus pro cerebro habes.	That's food for thought.	You have shit for brains.
Futue te ipsum et caballum in quo vectus est.	I take my hat off to you.	Screw you and the horse you rode in on.

USEFUL BUSINESS EXPRESSIONS

Take the bull by the horns.
Prehende taurum per cornua.

It comes with the territory.
Mos est huius loci.

Give me a little feedback.
Responde paulum, quaeso, ad id quod proposui.

If it ain't broke, don't fix it.
Noli reficere quod non fractum est.

Get your ducks in a row.
Instrue omnes anates tuas in acie.

The ball is in your court.
Pila in area tua est.

I'm up the creek without a paddle.
In rivo fimi sine remo sum.

MAKING A COLD CALL

I'd like to bounce something off you.
Volo cognoscere quid de meo consilio sentias.

You seem like someone who knows a good thing when he
    sees it.
Tute videris esse homo qui noscat opportunitatem cum videat.

It's a once-in-a-lifetime opportunity.
Talis occasio rarissima est.

I'm sorry we couldn't do business.
Stercus pro cerebro habes.

THE UNA-MINUTIA MANAGER

Take a letter.
Scribe.

Xerox this.
Fac exemplar huius Xerographicum.

Hold my calls.
Cura ut nemo me per telephonium accedat.

I don't get headaches. I give them.
Dolores capitis non fero, sed affero.

The buck stops here.
Hoc est mihi curae.

There's no free lunch.
Nulla mensa sine impensa.

You're fired.
Ego te demitto.

MOGUL JARGON

Let's take a meeting.
Congrediamur.

Have your people talk to my people.
Iube tuos colloqui cum meis.

What's the net-net on this?
Quid in re reditum residuum reliquumque restat?

It's the standard deal.
Condiciones consuetae sunt.

Baby, sweetheart, would I lie to you?
Amicule, deliciae, num mentiar tibi?

Let's cut to the chase.
Praefationem praeteramus.

Don't pass on this!
Noli praeterire hoc!

Give me a green light!
Ostende mihi lumen viride!

You're beautiful!
Pulcher es!

Let's have lunch, really!
Certe, prandeamus!

AURELIAN WALL STREET LATIN

Greed is good.
Avaritia est bonum.

The name of the game is leverage.
Lusus cum pecunia mutua sumpta tibi ludendus est.

I am a Master of the Universe!
Magister Universi sum!

I'm taking the Fifth!
Cito Emendationem Quintam!

IV.
RECREATIONAL LATIN
Lingua Latina Oblectamentis

AT THE FOOTBALL STADIUM

These are great seats, aren't they?
Nonne praestant haec sedilia?

First and ten, do it again! Touchdown!
Primum et decem! Iterum agendum! Transactum!

God, these halftime shows are boring.
*Hercle, haec ludicra inter dimidia muneris intercedentia insulsa
    sunt.*

We had a wardrobe malfunction!
Lapsum vestitus passi sumus!

CLASSICAL CHEERS FOR YOUR LOCAL COLOSSEUM

DEEE-fense!
DeFENNNNN-sio!

AAAAASSSSSS-hole!
CUUUUUUU-le!

Two, four, six, eight—who do we appreciate?
Duo, quattor, sex, octo—cui multum tribuimus?

Na na na na, na na na na, hey-hey, hey-hey-ey good-bye!
Nae nae nae nae, nae nae nae nae, heia-heia, vale!

LATIN CHEERS FOR THE IVY LEAGUE

Pursue them, pursue them, make them relinquish the ball!
Sequimini, sequimini, facite ut pilam relinquant!

Repel them, expel them, compel them to retreat!
Illos repellite, expellite, compellite ad fugiendum!

Oh, would that we would score!
Utinam vincamus!

We have been wanting and shall continue to want a
    touchdown!
Volebamus atque volemus pilam trans metas deponi!

AT THE BALL PARK

I hate Astroturf.
Gramen Artificiosum odi.

The designated-hitter rule has got to go.
Lex clavatoris designati rescindenda est.

The best baseball stadium is still Fenway Park.
Stadium sedipilae optimum Saeptum Paludosum etiamnunc est.

YOGI BERRA'S CELEBRATED SAYINGS ARE EVEN MORE IMMORTAL IN LATIN

When you come to a fork in the road, take it.
Cum ad bivium advenis, perge iter.

Nobody goes there anymore—it's too crowded.
Nemo ad illam tabernam nunc adit—semper enim cenatorum turba nimium stipatur.

If people don't want to come out to the ballpark, you can't stop them.
Si homines ad campum lusorium venire nolunt, eis obstare non potes.

The game of baseball is 90 percent mental, the other half is physical.
Ludendi pila clavaque novem partes in viribus mentis consistunt, dimidium alterum in viribus corporis.

If you can't imitate him, don't copy him.
Quem imitari non potes, noli simulare.

You can observe a lot just by watching.
Multum observare potes observare solum spectando.

If the world were perfect, it wouldn't be.
Si esset vita nostra emendata, non vero esset.

The future ain't what it used to be.
Futura non sunt eadem quae quondam fuerunt.

I never said most of the things I said.
Ex dictis meis, pleraque numquam dixi.

It ain't over 'til it's over.
Imperfectum est dum conficiatur.

LITTLE LEAGUE LATIN

We want a pitcher, not a glass of water!
Egemus iaculatore, non Iacchi latore!

Swings like a rusty gate!
Agitat tamquam ianua robiginosa!

He couldn't hit his baby brother!
Fratrem parvulum non posset ferire!

Swing, batter!
Pelle, percutor!

Strike out!
Eliditur!

LATIN CHATTER FOR THE INFIELD

Whaddya say, whaddya say, whaddya say!
Quid dicis, quid dicis, quid dicis!

Come on, baby, come on, baby!
Age, bone, age, bone!

Put it in there, put it in there!
Impone illuc, impone illuc!

Hey hey, say say!
Sic sic, dic dic!

Easy out, easy out, easy out!
Exactio facilis, exactio facilis, exactio facilis!

No batter, no batter, no batter!
Nihil tundit, nihil tundit, nihil tundit!

All right, all right! Way to go, way to go!
Bene, bene! Eugepae, eugepae!

AT A HOCKEY GAME

Hockey fans are real animals.
Adsectatores campylobactropaegnii vero bestiales sunt.

Here comes the Zamboni.
Huc accedit Zambonis.

ON THE GOLF COURSE

I'm going to take a mulligan.
Alterum ictum faciam.

We're playing winter rules, aren't we?
Nonne lege hiemali ludimus?

This is a gimme, isn't it?
Nonne hoc mihi conceditur?

Isn't that lucky? My ball just rolled out of the rough and onto
the fairway!
*Fortunatus sum! Pila mea de gramine horrido in pratum lene recta
modo volvit!*

ON THE TENNIS COURT

It's just out!
Paulo excessit!

A little wide!
Paulum extra finem!

It was just a hair long!
Longius capillo fuit!

It's out by an inch!
Una uncia abest!

ON THE SLOPES

Boy, I hate lift lines.
Heu, odi manere in agmine pro sellis volatilibus.

Watch where you're going, you jerk!
Vade cautius, cinaede!

Avalanche!
Lapsus nivium!

Let's get in the hot tub!
In thermulam intremus!

AT THE BEACH

Look at the hooters on that one.
Ecce illa mammeata.

Let's build a sand Forum.
Forum harenae aedificemus.

Do you want a frosty one?
Visne frigidum?

What's that in the water?
Quid est illud in aqua?

Shark! Shark!
Pistrix! Pistrix!

ON A YACHT

What happens if I pull this rope?
Quid fiat si hunc rudentum vellam?

Can I drive?
Licetne mihi gubernare?

Is there supposed to be a lot of water down here?
Oportetne multum aquae hic in ima nave esse?

All of a sudden I'm not feeling so good.
Subito minime valeo.

AT THE SPA

There is something wrong with this scale.
Haec trutina errat.

Was your masseur trained in East Germany?
Estne doctus tractator tuus in Germania Orientali?

It's on a plate, it must be food.
In catillo, iacet, nempe cibus est.

Is there an alcoholic beverage made from oat bran?
Estne ebriamen de furfure avenaceo factum?

V.
PRACTICAL LATIN
Lingua Latina Utilis

THINGS TO SAY TO YOUR LAWYER

Listen, would you repeat everything you just told me, only
    this time in English.
*Heu, quaeso itera omnia quae mihi modo narravisti, sed nunc
    Anglice.*

You charge how much an hour?
Quantum in singulas horas imputas?

THINGS TO SAY TO YOUR ACCOUNTANT

This amount here, is that what I made or what I owe?
Haec summa, estne quod merui an quod debeo?

Where do I sign?
Ubi signo?

THINGS TO SAY TO THE IRS AGENT

Unfortunately, I can't find those particular documents.
Eheu, litteras istas reperire non possum.

I know why the numbers don't agree! I use Roman numerals.
Scio cur summae inter se dissentiant! Numeris Romanis utor!

THINGS TO SAY TO YOUR BANKER

I don't want a toaster.
Tostrum panis non cupio.

I can't be overdrawn.
Fieri non potest ut ratio mea deficiat.

THINGS TO SAY TO YOUR STOCKBROKER

Just what exactly is a pork belly?
Quidnam est sterilicula?

I thought the idea was to buy low and sell high.
Credidi pretio parvo emere et magno vendere tibi in animo fuisse.

Are you telling me that sunspots caused the market crash?
Dicisne mihi maculas in sole omnia pretia simul iacere?

THINGS TO SAY TO YOUR DENTIST

This isn't going to hurt, is it?
Num mihi dolebit hoc?

Something important came up, so I'll have to cancel my
appointment.
*Quadam re magna instanta, necesse mihi est constitum tempus
demittere.*

THINGS TO SAY TO YOUR PSYCHIATRIST

Sometimes I get this urge to conquer large parts of Europe.
Interdum feror cupidine partium magnarum Europae vincendarum.

I think some people in togas are plotting against me.
Sentio aliquos togatos contra me conspirare.

I have this compulsion to speak Latin.
Nescioquid me Latine loqui cogit.

What has my mother got to do with it?
Quid agitur de matre mea?

THINGS TO SAY TO A TEENAGER

Really rad, dude!
Radicitus, comes!

What's happening?
Quid fit?

THINGS TO SAY TO AN OBNOXIOUS CHILD

In the good old days, children like you were left to perish on
    windswept crags.
Antiquis temporibus, nati tibi similes in rupibus ventosissimis
    exponebantur ad necem.

I'm rubber, you're glue, bounces off me, sticks to you!
*Quasi cummi sim elasticum, tuque gluten es, omnia quae blateras, a
me resilientia haerent ad te!*

THINGS TO SAY TO A MOVIE STAR

You look shorter and older in person.
Videris coram brevior corpore.

Can I have your autograph?
Scribe, sodes, dono mihi nomen tuum?

THINGS TO SAY TO THE HOI POLLOI

I do not have any spare change.
Non sunt mihi nummi subsicivi quos tibi donem.

I gave at the office.
In tabulario dona largitus sum.

I do not wish to "check it out."
Nolo id "perscrutari."

I'm not interested in your dopey religious cult.
Nihil curo de ista tua stulta superstitione.

If Caesar were alive, you'd be chained to an oar.
Si Caesar viveret, ad remum dareris.

THINGS TO SAY TO A MALFUNCTIONING SOFT-DRINK MACHINE

You infernal machine! Give me a beverage or give me back
my money!

*Machina improba! Aut ede mihi potum aut redde mihi meam
pecuniam!*

VI.
TACTICAL LATIN
Lingua Latina Rationi

EMBARRASSING SITUATIONS ARE LESS EMBARRASSING IN LATIN

I'd like to buy some condoms.
Volo comparare nonnulla prophylactica.

I didn't expect you home so soon!
Non sperabam te domum tam cito revenire!

I don't know how that got in my pocket.
Nescio quomodo illud in sinum meum intraverit.

Of course I know what day today is! I just can't remember
the English word for it.
*Scilicet scio qui dies sit hodiernus! Modo non possum meminisse
verbum Anglicum.*

Oh! I was just looking to see if you had any Kleenex here
among these papers on your desk.
*O! Conabar cognoscere num tibi adsit Nascida in mensa tua inter
haec scripta.*

Do you by any chance happen to own a large, yellowish, very
flat cat?
Estne tibi forte feles fulva magna planissima?

BALD-FACED LIES ARE LESS
BALD-FACED IN LATIN

The check is in the mail.
Perscriptio in manibus tabellariorum est.

I have nothing to declare.
Non est mihi quod declarem.

I don't know what you're talking about.
Nescio quid dicas.

It was that way when I got here.
Ita erat quando hic adveni.

There's no one here by that name.
Nemo adest, illius nominis hic.

Don't call me, I'll call you.
Noli me vocare, ego te vocabo.

FLATTERY SOUNDS MORE SINCERE IN LATIN

Have you lost weight?
Nonne minus obesus est?

You haven't aged a bit!
Minime senuisti!

It looks great on you!
Tibi multam affert venustatem!

A wig? I never would have guessed!
Capillamentum? Haudquaquam coniecissem!

INTIMATE SUBJECTS ARE EASIER TO BROACH IN LATIN

Your fly is open.
Braccae tuae hiant.

Your slip is showing.
Subucula tua apparet.

You have a big piece of spinach on your front teeth.
In dentibus primoribus frustum magnum spinaciae habes.

You've been misusing the subjunctive.
Abutebaris modo subiunctivo.

EXCUSES SOUND MORE BELIEVABLE IN LATIN

My dog ate it.
Canis meus id comedit.

The cleaning lady threw it away.
Ancilla id abiecit.

It fell into the shredder.
Inlapsum est in consectorem.

I did call. Maybe your answering machine is broken.
Sane ego te vocavi. Forsitan capedictum tuum desit.

My watch stopped.
Horologium manuale meum stitit.

My car wouldn't start.
Currus meus se movere noluit.

I was kidnapped by aliens. What year is it?
Extraterrestriales me abduxerunt. Qui annus est?

B.S. IS MORE CONVINCING IN LATIN

I'm glad you asked me that.
Gaudeo te illud de me rogavisse.

I'll put all my cards on the table.
Chartas meas omnes in tabulam ponam.

You know, I'm your biggest fan.
Edepol, fautor tuus maximus sum.

I'm only thinking of what's best for you.
Modo cogit quid prosit rebus tuis.

Believe me, this hurts me more than it hurts you.
Crede mihi, huius causa ego doleo magis quam doles tu.

SNOW JOBS ARE HOWLING BLIZZARDS IN LATIN

Your look is marvelous!
Quam pulcher/pulchra es.

How truly fascinating! Do tell me more!
Tua verba animum meum tenent! Te precor mihi plus enarrare!

That's simply divine!
Divinissimum est!

I had a grand time!
Me valde oblectavi.

I shall always cherish the memory of this very, very special
   occasion.
Semper redibo laetus hunc diem praecipuum in memoriam.

Perhaps a small obelisk could be erected to commemorate it.
Forsitan nobis deceat statuere obeliscum parvum ad rem
   celebrandum.

YOU CAN SELL PRACTICALLY ANYBODY PRACTICALLY ANYTHING IN LATIN

Tell you what I'm going to do . . .
Mihi permitte tibi dicere quod faciam . . .

This is a rock-bottom price.
Hoc est pretium minimum.

I'm losing money on this deal.
Hoc pacto, pecuniam amitto.

My boss will kill me when he finds out.
Praefectus me a medio tollet quando cognoverit.

Sign here.
Hic signa.

Next!
Propinqua proxime!

LATIN MEDICAL NAMES FOR NONEXISTENT BUT USEFUL DISEASES

Impedimentum memoriae
(A mental block that makes it hard for you to remember
    names)

Inopia celeritatis
(A mild dyslexia that makes it impossible to arrive on time)

Dolor anteprandialis
(A gastric problem that occasionally makes you cancel a
    lunch)

Morbus irrigatonis
(A rare disease aggravated by watering friends' plants)

Taedium pellucidorum
(An eye condition that keeps you from looking at people's
    slides)

AN ALL-PURPOSE EVASION OF A REQUEST FOR A LATIN TRANSLATION

You can't say that in Latin.
Illud Latine dici non potest.

AN ALL-PURPOSE PHONY TRANSLATION OF A LATIN INSCRIPTION

"Having done these things, they made the sacrifices prescribed by custom lest they be found lacking in filial piety."

VII.
CULTURAL LATIN
Lingua Latina Docta

AT THE THEATER

If you want good tickets, you've got to go to a scalper.
Si desideras tesseras bonas tibi opus est ad sectorum ire.

You know, we really ought to go to the theater more often.
Pol, ad spectaculum saepius ire nobis libebit.

Fire!
Flamma!

AT A CONCERT

What time do you think we'll be out of here?
Qua hora credis nos exituros?

Is it over? Do I applaud now?
Estne peractus concertus? Nuncine plaudo?

AT A LITERARY GATHERING

Seen any good movies lately?
Vidistine nuper aliqua spectacula cinematographica bona?

How about those Forty-Niners?
Quid sentis de Undequinquagesimariis?

AT A POETRY READING

It doesn't rhyme.
Nullo metro compositum est.

I don't care. If it doesn't rhyme, it isn't a poem.
Non curo. Si metrum non habet, non est poema.

AT AN ART EXHIBITION

You call this art? A two-year-old could do better.
*Dicisne hoc opus artificiosum esse? Quivis infans melius facere
     potest.*

I don't know much about art, but I know what I like.
Cum artis peritus non sim, nosco quod amo.

AT THE MOVIES

This is a remake of a French film.
Haec imago movens ex priore Gallica recreata est.

The sequel is never as good as the original.
Sequella numquam tam bona est quam originalis.

Look out, there's some crud on this seat.
Cave, est aliquod squaloris in hac sede.

TIMELESS LINES FROM THE MOVIES

Make my day.
Perge, ut hunc diem appelem beatum.

Round up the usual suspects.
Conlige solitos haberi suspectos.

You know, Toto, I have a feeling we're not in Kansas
   anymore.
Certe, Toto, sentio nos in Kansate non iam esse.

Frankly, my dear, I don't give a damn.
Ut plane dicam, cara mea, flocci non facio.

THE LATIN DIALOGUE YOU MISSED IN MEL GIBSON'S *PASSION*

Blood, gore, good guys, bad guys, and plenty of ooga-
   booga—boy, this is going to make a heck of a movie in
   about 2000 years!
*Ecce sanguis, cruor, homines boni malique, mira multa edepol—ex
   his fiet post duo milia ferme annorum spectaculum
   cinematographicum memoria dignissimum!*

The Romans killed Christ—let's go torch a pizzeria!
*Romani cruci Christum—fixerunt ergo incendamus libarium
   Neapolitanum!*

Seen one lashing, seen 'em all, but, holy moly, did you get a
   load of those frigging nails?
Una verberatione visa, satis est imago verberationis cognita, sed
   mehercule, conspexistine istos clavos magnos et diros?

All that because of a couple of lousy sermons? Man, what
   would those clowns do to you if you did something really
   bad, like call the Emperor a buttwipe?
Haecine omnia propter paucos sermones? Eheu! Si quis grave
   maleficium committat, quali poena eum multent ista propudia
   si, exempli gratia, Imperatorem vocet irrumatorem?

Pontius Pilate, he's our man!—If he can't do it, nobody can!
Pontius Pilatus, dux noster est!—Si non potest ille, nemo potest!

I've got a great idea for a sequel—Starsky and Christ!
Spectaculum sequens optimum animo concepi—appellabitur
   Starscius et Christus!

Oy vey! Are we going to catch a lot of crap for this!
Vae! Huius causa, in capita nostra multa merda manabit!

ALL MUSIC IS CLASSICAL MUSIC IN LATIN

My favorite group is . . .
Caterva quam diligo maxime est . . .

The Beatles
Cimictus

The Temptations
Illecebrae

The Rolling Stones
Lapides Provolventes

The Who
To Tines

The Grateful Dead
Manes Grati

The Monkees
Simitatores

The Beach Boys
Pueri Litorales

Country Joe and the Fish
Iosephus Agrestis Piscesque

ALL TV IS EDUCATIONAL TV IN LATIN

My favorite show is
Spectaculum quod diligo maxime est . . .

Gilligan's Island
Insula Gilliganis

Hawaii Five-O
Hawaii Quinque-Nil

Hollywood Squares
Quadrata Iliceti

The Gong Show
Spectaculum Tintinnabuli

The Love Boat
Navis Amoris

The Price Is Right
Pretium Iustum Est

Leave It to Beaver
Id Castori Concedite

Jeopardy
Periculum

Mission: Impossible
Opus: Quod Fieri Non Potest

Wheel of Fortune
Rota Fortunae

Diff'rent Strokes
Ictus Diff'rentes

Divorce Court
Curia Divortiorum

Happy Days
Dies Felices

The Flintstones
Silices

The Young and the Restless
Iuvenes Inquietesque

The Twilight Zone
Zona Crepusculi

VIII.
SOCIAL LATIN
Lingua Latina Vitae Communi

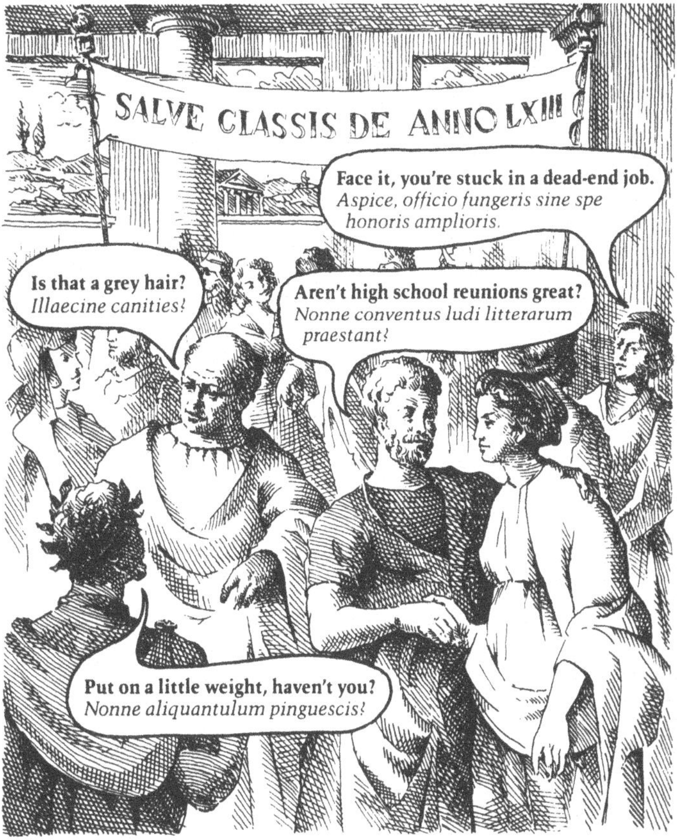

IN A BAR

I'll have . . .
Da mihi sis . . .

> a light beer.
> *cerevisiam dilutam.*

> a glass of white wine.
> *poculum vini albi.*

> a martini.
> *spiculum argentum.*

> a fog cutter.
> *quod nebulam dissipat.*

I'll drink to that!
Hoc ei propinabo!

Bartender! Another round!
Caupo! Fer etiam potus omnibus!

Cheers!
Propino tibi salutem!

AT A WASP COUNTRY CLUB

That is the largest drink I have ever seen.
Illa potio maxima est a me visa.

I think several of the people here are dead.
Credo nonnullos hic mortuos esse.

Those green pants go so well with that pink shirt and the
plaid jacket!
*Braccae illae virides cum subucula rosea et tunica Caledonia—
quam eleganter concinnatur!*

I can't understand what you are saying. Are your jaws wired
together?
*Verba tua intellegere non possum. Filone ferreo maxillae tuae iuncta
sunt?*

AT A HIP DISCO

Do you want to dance? I know the Funky Broadway.
Visne saltare? Viam Latam Fungosam scio.

How do you get your hair to do that?
Quomodo cogis comas tuas sic stare?

AT A BIRTHDAY PARTY

Happy Birthday!
Tibi diem natalem felicem!

Here's a pinch to grow an inch!
Te vellico ut uncia crescas!

Speech! Speech!
Ora! Ora!

AT A FAMILY REUNION

Put on a little weight, haven't you?
Nonne aliquantulum pinguescis?

Is that a gray hair?
Illaecine canities?

Honey/buster, when are you going to get married?
*Mellita/comes, quando aliquem/aliquam in matrimonium
    accipies/duces?*

You're not going to get a divorce, are you?
Num est tibi in animo divortium facere?

Face it, you're stuck in a dead-end job.
Aspice, officio fungeris sine spe honoris amplioris.

Say, you sure are drinking a lot.
Ra vera, potas bene.

Isn't it great to have the whole family together?
Nonne dulce est familiam totam in unum locum cogere?

AT YOUR HIGH SCHOOL REUNION

Oh! Was I speaking Latin again?
Vah! Denuone Latine loquebar?

Silly me. Sometimes it just sort of slips out.
O ineptum. Interdum modo haec loquela elabitur.

TALKING TO PETS

Polly want a cracker?
Pulle! Visne frustrum?

Sit! Roll over! You see, he understands Latin.
Sede! Volve! Ecce, Latine scit.

Bad kitty! Why don't you use the cat box? I put new litter
in it.
Feles mala! Cur cista non uteris? Stramentum novum in ea posui.

USEFUL CURSES

May barbarians invade your personal space!
Utinam barbari spatium proprium tuum invadant!

May conspirators assassinate you in the mall!
Utinam coniurati te in foro interficiant!

May faulty logic undermine your entire philosophy!
Utinam logica falsa tuam philosophiam totam suffodiant!

May you always misuse the subjunctive!
Utinam modo subiunctivo semper abutaris!

THE FINE PRINT IS EVEN FINER IN LATIN

Batteries not included.
Lagunculae Leydianae non accedunt.

Void where prohibited by law.
Inritum est ubicumque legibus prohibitum est.

Some restrictions may apply.
Forsitan ad hoc aliquot condiciones pertineant.

Substantial penalty for early withdrawal.
Poenas magnas ob depositum praemature postulatum expetimus.

THINGS YOU SAY IN YOUR SLEEP SOUND LESS RIDICULOUS IN LATIN

I forgot to polish the clocks!
Oblitus sum perpolire clepsydras!

Where's my rubber ducky?
Ubi est mea anaticula cumminosa?

Uh-oh, here comes the lobster man!
Eheu, horsum venit vir qui fert locustas!

Shower shoes! Shower shoes! Shower shoes!
Crepidae balneariae! Crepidae balneariae! Crepidae balneariae!

CERTAIN REQUESTS ARE MORE TACTFULLY COMMUNICATED IN LATIN

Bite my crank.
Morde manubrium meum.

Eat my shorts.
Vescere bracis meis.

Put it where the sun don't shine.
Pone ubi sol non lucet.

BIOLOGICAL TERMS OF ENDEARMENT

Homo sapiens
A human being

Fiber fervidus
An eager beaver

Cuniculus inscius
A dumb bunny

Pavo perfectus
A total turkey

Lacertus atrioli
A lounge lizard

Fera festiva
A party animal

Radix lecti
A couch potato

IX.
SENSUAL LATIN
Lingua Latina Libidinosa

STARTING A RELATIONSHIP

Do you come here often?
Venisne saepe huc?

Haven't we met somewhere before?
Nonne alicui prius convenimus?

What's your sign?
Quo signo nata es?

You strike me as a very deep person.
Apparet te habere ingenium profundum.

I feel that I already know you.
Sentio me iam te novisse.

I think fate brought us together.
Credo fatum nos coegisse.

Your place or mine?
Apudne te vel me?

PILLOW TALK IS MORE ORIGINAL IN LATIN

How was it for you?
Quantum placui tibi?

Did the earth move?
Movitne terra, ut ita dicam?

Was I great, or what?
Nonne fui magnificus?

Want to do it again?
Visne iterum agere?

HAVING A RELATIONSHIP

You know, the Romans invented the art of love.
Romani quidem artem amatoriam invenerunt.

A little more up and to the right.
Paululum sursum et dextrosum.

Oh! More! Go on! Yes! Ooh! Ummm!
O! Plus! Perge! Aio! Hui! Hem!

ENDING THE RELATIONSHIP

Let's not rush into anything.
In ullam rem ne properemus.

I'm not ready to make a commitment.
Non sum paratus me committere.

I'm not sure we're right for each other.
Nescio num alius idoneus alii sit.

I hope we'll still be friends.
Spero nos familiares mansuros.

I guess fate wanted us to part.
Suspicor fatum nos voluisse diversos.

A CHECKERED PAST IS EASIER TO REVEAL IN LATIN

I've been married before.
Matrimonio priore cum altera olim iunctus sum.

This isn't my real name.
Hoc nomen meum verum non est.

I spent some time in prison.
Spatium temporis in carcere egi.

I don't really know all that much Latin.
Re vera, linguam Latinam vix cognovi.

X.

GASTRONOMICAL LATIN

Lingua Latina Cenatica

Give me a hamburger, french fries, and a thick shake.
Da mihi sis bubulae frustum assae, solana tuberosa in modo Gallico fricta, ac quassum lactatum coagulatum crassum.

The waitress drew a smiley face on the check.
Ancilla in computatione faciem subridentem pinxit.

THINGS TO SAY IN A FAST-FOOD RESTAURANT

I'll have . . .
Da mihi sis . . .

> a hamburger, french fries, and a thick shake.
> *bubulae frustum assae, solana tuberosa in modo Gallico fricta ac
>   quassum lactatum coagulatum crassum.*

> a bucket of fried chicken.
> *hamam carnis gallinaceae frictae.*

> a pizza with everything on it.
> *crustum Etruscum cum omnibus in eo.*

THINGS TO SAY IN A CHAIN THEME RESTAURANT

I want the buffalo chicken wings.
Alas gallinaceas buffaloenses cupio.

The waitress drew a smiley face on my check.
Ancilla in computatione faciem subridentum pinxit.

THINGS TO SAY IN A CHINESE RESTAURANT

Please, no MSG.
Parce, sodes, glutamoto monosodio.

Do you have "flied lice?" Ha ha ha.
Habesne "olyzam flictam?" Hae hae hae.

THINGS TO SAY IN A PRETENTIOUS RESTAURANT

Frankly, I think the chef put too much thyme in the sauce.
Ut verum dicam, credo coquum nimium thymi in liquamen misisse.

Look at the size of that pepper mill.
Ecce magnitudinem illae molae piperis.

It's a nice little wine but it lacks character and depth.
Vinum bellum iucundumque est, sed animo corporeque caret.

THINGS TO SAY WHILE BARBEQUING

Take a look at those steaks!
Contemplare carunculas illas!

You've really got to soak the charcoal with fuel.
Necesse est carbones igne Graeco madefacere.

The mosquitos are murder tonight!
Culices pessimi hac nocte sunt!

Ever noticed how wherever you stand, the smoke goes right in your face?
Animadvertistine, ubicumque stes, fumum recta in faciem ferri?

Come and get it!
Venite ac capite!

THINGS TO SAY TO THE MAÎTRE D' WHEN YOU DON'T HAVE A RESERVATION

Could you check again? My name must be there.
Inspice, sodes, denuo. Certo scio nomen adesse.

I don't understand. My secretary called a week ago.
Non intellego. Scriba mea te per filum vocavit septem diebus ante.

Listen, I have a very important business client with me.
Audi, mecum habeo socium in negotiis magni momenti.

He's also my oldest friend.
Insuper etiam est amicus veterrimus.

It's both of our birthdays.
Haec est nobis ambobus dies natalis.

I'm a restaurant reviewer.
Cauponas percenseo.

Here's ten bucks.
Ecce, tibi do decem Ioachimicos.

Pretty please with cherry on top!
Te precor dulcissime supplex!

AT THE STOP 'N' SHOP—*GAUDEAT EMPTOR!* (LET THE BUYER REJOICE!)

Jelly beans
Fabae suaves

Twinkies
Scintillae

Fish sticks
Piscilli

Gummy bears
Ursuli Gumminosi

Tinfoil
Bractea stannea

Sloppy Joes
Iosephi Inconditi

Bubble gum
Manducabulla

Glad Bags
Sacci Laeti

Fig Newtons
Crustula Ficulnea

Mars bars
Lateres Martiales

Shake 'n Bake
Quate et Coque

Chips Ahoy
Ave Assulae

Milky Ways
Viae Lacteae

Roast 'n Boast
Torre ac Gloriare

Handy Wipes
Mantelia Habilia

Moon Pie
Crusta Lunaria

Pop Tarts
*Scriblitae
   Exsilientes*

Ty-D-Bol
Matula Nitida

Pretzels
Nodi salsi

Devil Dogs
Crusti Diaboli

Sweet 'N Low
Dulce Leveque

Potato chips
*Assulae solanorum
   tuberosum*

Rice-a-Roni
Oryza Mixta

Tender Vittles
Esca Tenera

Kibbles 'n Bits
Frusta et Gustula

Cheese Whiz
Caseus Velox

Tuna Helper
Adiutor Thunni

Pampers
Indulgentes

| Miracle Whip | Yard Guard |
| *Confusio Mirifica* | *Custodia Propatuli* |

Roach Motels	
Cauponae	Jujubes
Blattariae	*Zizypha*

THE OLDEST JINGLES SOUND BRAND-NEW IN LATIN

Double your pleasure, double your fun, with double good,
double fresh Doublemint gum!
Duplica gaudia tua et delectamenta, bis bona, bis nova, gummi
Diplomentha!

Hold the pickles, hold the lettuce! Special orders don't upset
us, at McDonald's!
Parce cucumeris frustis! Parce lactucae! Mandata perculiaria nobis
non sunt oneri, apud Filtum Donaldi!

Call Roto-Rooter—that's the name—and away go troubles
down the drain!
Vocate Purgatorem Versabundum—nomen est nobis—et in cloacas
abluemus calamitates quae sunt vobis!

A ROMAN RECIPE

1. Get 1,000 larks.
2. Remove tongues and set aside.
3. Discard the larks.

I. *Alaudarum M cape.*
II. *Linguas excesa et sepone.*
III. *Alaudas abice.*

4. Put tongues in pan with oil and and sauté quickly.

IV. *Linguas mitte in sartaginem cum paulo olei et frigo cito.*

5. Transfer to hot platter. Serves 4.

V. *Eas traice ad patellam calidam. Quattor sufficit.*

FOOD FOR THOUGHT: ROMANCE LANGUAGE MENU ALERT

horse	*caballus*
goat	*capra*
rabbit	*cuniculus*
brains	*cerebelli*
eel	*anguilla*
sea eels	*congri*
sea snails	*bucina*
sea slugs	*limaces*
lampreys	*lampredae*

XI.

FAMILIAL LATIN

Lingua Latina Domestica

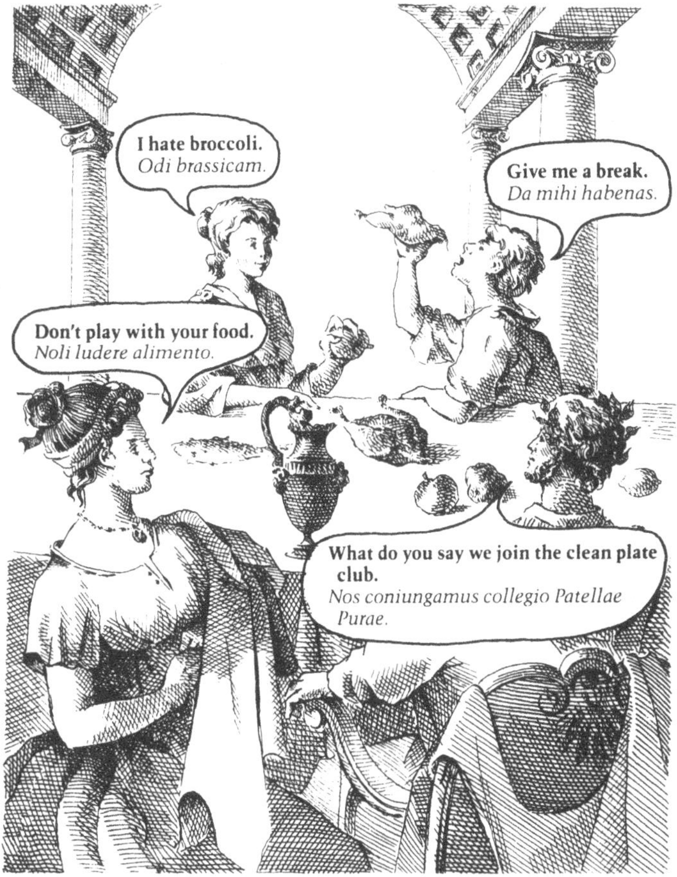

DOMESTIC DISCOURSE

Honey, I'm home.
Mellila, domi adsum.

Sheesh, what a day!
Mehercle, qualis dies!

You did what to the car?
Quid carrus passus est?

You paid how much for that dress?
Quantum illae stolae pependisti?

Something's burning.
Aliquid ardet.

Oh, no, it's the roast, and the boss is coming to dinner!
Vae, ardet assa bubula atque patronus ad cenam veniet!

MINOR MISUNDERSTANDINGS

Shopping list? What shopping list?
Libellus comparandorum? Qui libellus comparandorum?

I thought you were going to pick up the kids.
Credidi te liberos colligere.

Don't ask me where the keys are. You had them last.
Noli me rogare ubi sint claves. Tu eas nunc nuper habebas.

But you told me your mother was coming *next* month!
Sed me docuisti matrem tuam postero *mense venturam esse!*

A call from someone named "Bubbles"? It's a wrong number.
Vocatusne de quadam "Bullula" nomine? Numerus falsus est.

TABLE TALK

My favorite! Tuna noodle casserole!
Mea dilectissima! Farrago thunni!

What do you say we join the clean-plate club?
Nos coniungamus collegio patellae purae?

You'll eat it and like it, or you'll have it for breakfast
    tomorrow.
Aut id devorabis amabisque, aut cras prandebis.

Don't play with your food! Remember the starving
    Carthaginians!
Noli ludere alimento! Memento Carthaginienses esurientes!

LAYING DOWN THE LAW

This report card is a disgrace.
Haec renuntiatio infamis est.

Pay attention! I'm speaking to you!
Ausculta mihi! Tibi dico!

You're grounded!
Ad domum adligaris!

No TV for a week!
Nullam televisionem spectabis per septimanam!

I'm cutting your allowance in half!
Peculium dimidiatum est!

When I was your age . . .
Cum tam iuvenis eram quam nunc es . . .

> I had a full-time job in a salt mine.
> *in salinis octo horas in dies laborabam.*

> I won the Nobel Prize for promptness and neatness.
> *Praemium Nobelium celeritatis et munditiae abstuli.*

> I could speak Latin.
> *Latine loqui poteram.*

TOUGH TALK

N-O spells No!
Verbum non N-O-N scribitur!

Nothing doing, and that's final.
Haud fiet, et clavo fixum est.

I don't care what the other parents are doing.
Curae mihi non est quod alii parentes faciant.

I am not being unreasonable.
Non sum iniquus.

All right, we'll ask your mother.
Bene, matrem tuam rogabimus.

Okay, just this once.
Ita, semel et solum tibi permissum est.

DISCUSSING THE BABYSITTER

I think she's from another planet.
Arbitror eam de planeta alia venisse.

Did her parents drop her off here in a spacecraft?
Astroscaphane parentes eam huc portaverunt?

Maybe she's just a drug addict.
Fortasse modo opio addicta est.

I think I've seen her face on a milk carton or down at the post office.
Credo me faciem suam in olla lactis vel in tabulario tabellariorum vidisse.

IN THE MEN'S DEPARTMENT

This suit looks a little baggy.
Vestimentum laxum paululum videtur.

The lapels are too wide.
Fimbriae latiores sunt.

I don't like this shade.
Colorem hunc non diligo.

Honey, what do you think?
Mellila, quid sentis?

When will it be ready?
Quando praesto fiet?

ON THE ROAD

We ought to have made that turn.
Nos opertuit tunc vertisse.

Give me the map.
Da mihi chartam.

Let's ask directions.
Aliquem de via consulamus.

Would you like me to drive?
Visne me currum agere?

I am not lost.
Neutiquam ero.

Settle down back there.
Sedate vos, posteriores.

Why didn't you go when you had the chance?
Cur non isti mictum ex occasione?

You'll just have to hold it in.
Opus est tibi urinam inhibere.

Next time you'll take the bus.
Carru Canis Cani veharis posthac.

XII.
FORMAL LATIN
Lingua Latina Ritibus

AT A BLACK-TIE DINNER PARTY

Let's switch place cards.
Chartas loci mutemus.

Is this the right fork?
Hacine furcilla uti decet?

Wait, that's my bread plate.
Siste, patella panis est mea.

Do I drink this or stick my fingers in it?
Bibamne hoc, an in id digitos inseram?

My dessert is on fire!
Mensa secunda mea flagrat!

AT A WEDDING

It's not too late to back out!
Non serius matrimonium fugias.

AT A CHRISTENING

Do you ever worry that there was a mix-up at the hospital?
Vobisne curae umquam est num in valetudinario confusio facta sit?

AT A FUNERAL

Remember when we only used to run into each other at
    weddings?
Meministine cum nos solum in nuptiis obviam eramus?

LATIN IS ALWAYS ACCEPTABLE IN
POLITE COMPANY

Who cut the cheese?
Quisnam pepedit?

Catch that and sew a button on it!
Illud cape et ei fibulam adfige!

Excuse me, I've got to go take a dump.
Ignosce mihi, cacare necesse est.

Look out, I'm going to barf!
Cave, vomiturus sum!

FINAL LATIN

Denique diaetam efficacem inveni.
At last I have found a diet that works.

Nunc vero inter saxum et locum durum sum.
Now, I really am between a rock and a hard place.

Dixi me aegrotare sed ecquis auscultaret?
I said I was sick, but would anybody listen?

Tam exanimis quam tunica nehru sum
I am as dead as the Nehru jacket.

In vicem res bona est non plus dentharpagarum.
On the other hand, the good news is no more dentistry.

Sic friatur crustum dulce.
It is thus that the cookie crumbles.

Obesa cantavit.
The fat lady has sung.

XIII.
CASUAL LATIN
Lingua Latina Quotidiana

LATIN: IT'S MORE THAN A LANGUAGE—
IT'S AN ATTITUDE

Yes, I have a personal Latin trainer.
Aio, exercitorem linguae Latinae proprium habeo.

We're working on my ablative and subjunctives.
Exercemus casus ablativos et modos subjunctivos meos.

I want to get my syntax into shape for the beach this summer.
Volo ut syntaxis mea splendescat in litore, veniente aestate.

THE BASIC PHILOSOPHIES ARE BEST
EXPRESSED IN LATIN

I think, therefore I am.
Cogito, ergo sum.

I am, therefore I eat.
Sum, ergo edo.

I think, therefore I am depressed.
Cogito, ergo doleo.

I think I'll have another drink.
Cogito sumere potum alterum.

ALL BOOKS ARE GREAT BOOKS IN LATIN

Princess Daisy
Regis Filia Composita

Valley of the Dolls
Valles Puparum

Once Is Not Enough
Semel Non Satis Est

Smart Women, Foolish Choices
Mulieres Sapientes, Optantes Ineptae

Living, Loving, and Learning
Vivere, Amare, Discere

I'm OK—You're OK
Valeo—Vales

*Everything You Always Wanted to Know About Sex but Were
    Afraid to Ask*
*Omnia Quae De Rebus Venereis Cognoscere Semper Voluisti sed
    Rogare Metuisti*

SNIPPETS OF POETRY ARE EASIER TO WEDGE INTO THE CONVERSATION IN LATIN

A rose is a rose is a rose.
Rosa rosa rosa est est.

Do I dare to eat a peach?
Audeone persicum edere?

Not with a bang but a whimper.
Non crepitu, sed vagitu.

Quoth the Raven, "Nevermore!"
Dixit Corvus, "Numquam postea!"

DOPEY EXPRESSIONS ARE MORE FORCEFUL IN LATIN

Go with the flow.
Ventis secundis, tene cursum.

Don't let the bastards wear you down.
Noli nothis permittere te terere.

Lead, follow, or get out of the way.
Duc, sequere, aud de via decede.

Let it all hang out.
Totum dependeat.

THERE IS NO SUCH THING AS A STUPID QUESTION IN LATIN

What, in a nutshell, is deconstructionism?
Paucis verbis, quid est deconstructionismus?

Who exactly are the Kurds?
Quinam sunt Carduchi?

If you put a little pyramid on top, does that make something
    postmodern?
Si in culmine pyramidem parvum superponis, ita fit aliquid
    postneotericum?

YOUR TWO CENTS' WORTH GOES A LOT FARTHER IN LATIN

I'd much rather have a '55 Thunderbird than a '58 Corvette.
Magnopere malim Tonitravem anni MCMLV quam Corvettam anni
    MCMLVIII.

Ali could have beaten Tyson.
Ali Tysonem vicesset, si pugnavissent.

You really shouldn't keep a dog in the city.
Canis in urbe custodiendus non est.

All frozen pizzas taste lousy.
Omnes lagani pistrinae gelati male sapiunt.

You can't get a decent sound system for under a grand.
Non potest composituram machinarum quae apte musicam faciunt
    emere minoris quam mille.

LATIN FOR LAS VEGAS

Are these slots progressive?
Crescuntne gradatim praedae ab his latronibus unibrachiis?

I hit the jackpot!
Copiam cepi!

Come on, baby needs a new pair of shoes!
Age, infanti opus est pari novorum calceorum!

Damn! Snake eyes!
Vae! Canes!

A fresh deck please, and cut 'em thin to win!
*Sis, fer sarcinam recentem chartularum, et parti illas impariter ut
    praedas paremus!*

LATIN FOR THE LOTTERY

Do you have any tickets with Roman numerals?
Habesne ullas tesseras numeris Romanis impressas?

No wonder I never win!
Non miror me numquam vicisse!

XIV.
PERSONAL LATIN
Lingua Latina Propria

LATIN: THE PERFECT PREPPY PATOIS

Let's mix up a pitcher of Bloodys, get crocked, and drop trou!
In urceo numerum Sanguineorum misceamus, ebrii fiamus et bracas demittamus!

Excellent! Intense quaffing action!
Praestantem! Nunc est adsiduo perpotandum!

Major party bore! Biff's going to toss his tacos!
Taedium convivii maius! Bartholomaeus vomiturus est!

He has to drive the big white bus to Woof City!
Sibi necesse est agere magnam raedam albam ad Municipium Eiectamenti!

Let's bolt!
Evolemus!

We're golden!
Aurei sumus!

LATIN: THE ULTIMATE YUPPIE LINGO

My Rolex is waterproof to twelve hundred meters.
Rolex meum vim aquae potest resistere usque ad altitudinem trium milium septingentorum pedum.

I have a fax machine in my BMW.
In curru meo ab Officina Baiuoaria Mechanica fabricato habeo machinam quae litteras per aethera transmittit.

I know a restaurant with only one table.
Novi cauponam quae solum unam mensam habet.

My jogging suit is by Armani.
Armanius vestitum cursorium meum fecit.

My Jacuzzi is filled with Perrier.
Meum balineum calidum verticosum cum aqua scintillante fontana Gallica impletum est.

My bankruptcy lawyer is Alan Dershowitz.
Ego decoctor iuris consulto Alano Dershowitzi utor.

GOLDEN AGE LATIN FOR NEW-AGE PEOPLE

Pyramids are out. I'm putting all my crystals in a little domed box shaped like the Pantheon.
Pyramides obsoletae sunt. Servo omnes gemmas crystallinas meas in cista formata in tholum instar Pantheonis.

Using the subjunctive generates more alpha waves than meditation.
Modus subiunctivus gignit plus fluctuum alpha quam meditatio.

Obviously your id, ego, and libido are going to be able to
   express themselves more fully in their native language—
   Latin.
*Manifesto id, ego, et libidino poterunt plenius se declarare lingua
   indigena—Latina videlicet.*

Roman numerology is a thousand years older than
   Johnny-come-lately systems based on Arabic squiggles.
*Vaticinatio quae numeris Romanis utitur vetustior est milibus annis
   quam ulla ratio sera quae scriptis Arabicis utitur.*

Om . . .
Omo   Omamus
Omas   Omatus
Omat   Omant

LATIN IS ALWAYS POLITICALLY CORRECT

I sing of arms and a dead white male.
Arma virumque cano flavum qui nunc est mortuus.

I came, I saw, I spoke out on a number of critical Third World
   issues.
*Veni, vidi, verba fecide pluribus gravibus pertinentibus ad Partem
   Tertiam Orbis Terrarum, quae, ut scis, in partes tres divisa est.*

Languages that don't have separate genders are sexist.
Linguae quae genera distincta non habent inuriam faciunt feminis!

Let us firmly reject all commands, conditions, and
   prohibitions that are not expressed in the subjunctive!
*Repudiemus obstinate omnia mandata et condiciones et interdicta
   quae in modo subiunctivo non expressa sint!*

TIBER VALLEY GIRL

I'm, you know, in the mall, and I'm like talking to this major
   studmuffin?
Sum enim in foro, et modo, en, loquor cum quodam Adonide mero?

It was totally awesome—I mean, really copious rad!
Omnino mirabile fuit—volo dicere, vero probe radictus!

And then I had negative clues, and I misused the subjunctive.
*Tum autem indicia mihi erant obscura, et modo subiunctivo abusa
   sum.*

What a buzzstomp! Multiple sadness! I was mega raked!
*O stridorem conculcatorum! Maestiam multiplicatam! Magnopere
   excruciata sum!*

Gag me with a spoon!
Si modo cochleario faceres me vomere!

FUNNY, YOU DON'T LOOK LATINISH

Oy vay, what a—
Eheu, qualem—

klutz!	kibitzer!
inhabilem!	*interpellatorem!*
schnook!	nebbish!
blennum!	*tenuiculum!*
schlemiel!	putz!
virum laevum!	*verpam!*
yenta!	momser!
oblatratricem!	*nothum!*
gonif!	schmuck!
furem!	*mentulam!*
schnorrer!	
parasitum!	

CHARIOTS OF THE ROMANS?

Okay, so if Plautus didn't write Shakespeare's plays, how
come so many of them are set in Italy?
*Si quidem, ut dicis, Plautus non scripsit Shakespearianas fabulas,
quamobrem tot ex illis actae sunt utentes scaena Italica?*

Did you ever ask yourself why all the craters on the moon have Latin names?

Rogavistine umquam te ipsum cur sint omnibus crateribus in luna nomina Latina?

Atlantis—Atlantic City. Think about it.

Atlantis—Urbs Atlantica. Cogita de hoc.

XV.
CONVIVIAL LATIN
Lingua Latina Hilaris

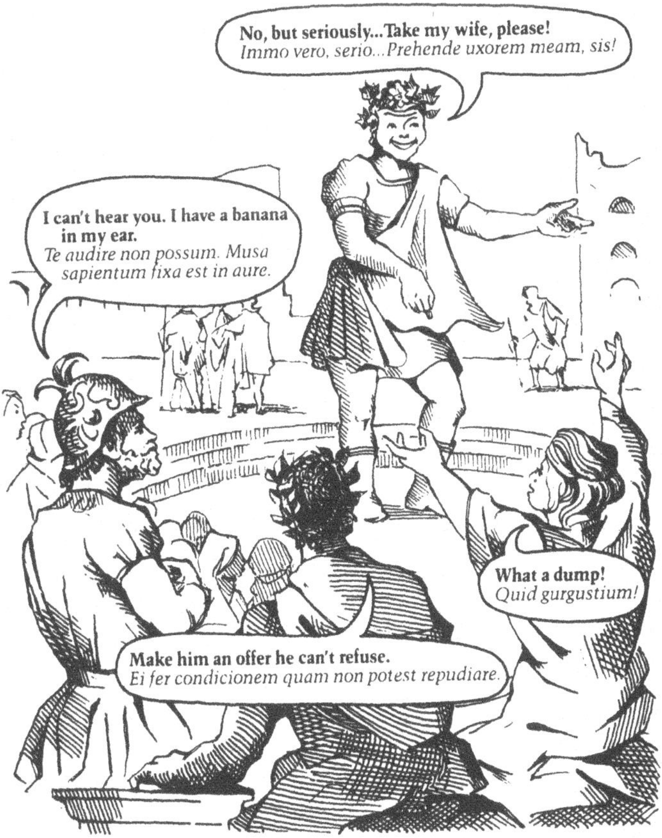

PUNCH LINES HAVE MORE PUNCH IN LATIN

I can't hear you. I have a banana in my ear.
Te audire non possum. Musa sapientum fixa est in aure.

You know, that dog isn't really all *that* shaggy.
Re vera, canis ille nequaquam adeo *pilosus est.*

And at these prices, you won't see many more kangaroos in
    this bar, either.
*Et tantis pretiis constitutis plures Macropodidas in hac caupona
    minime videbis.*

WISECRACKS ARE WISER IN LATIN

Is that a scroll in your toga, or are you just happy to see me?
Estne volumen in toga, an solum tibi libet me videre?

Take a picture, it lasts longer!
Fac imaginem, diutius durabit!

COMEDY NIGHT AT CAESAR'S PALACE

Take my wife, please!
Prehende uxorem meam, sis!

No, but seriously . . .
Immo vero, serio . . .

I just flew in from Gaul—boy, are my arms tired!
Nuperrime de Gallia huc volavi—Mehercle, bracchia mea defatigata sunt!

Anyone here from Rome?
Adestne quisquam de Roma?

Listen: I just got the latest score from the Colosseum—Lions 32, Christians 0, in sudden-death overtime!
Audite: Modo de Colosseo rationem interfectorum recentissimam cognovi—Leonibus triginta duo, Christianis nihil, clepsydra addita ad spatium mortis subitae!

Do you know how many barbarians it takes to light a torch? One million—one to hold the torch, and the rest to get together and try to discover fire!
Scitisne quantus numerus barbarorum satis est ut ipsi facem accendere possint? Decies centena milia—uno facem tenente, debent ceteri convenire atque conari ignem invenire!

You're just like my agent—you get ten percent of my jokes!
Simillimi procuratoris mei estis—iocorum meorum partem decimam prehenditis!

But really, you've been a beautiful audience! I love ya, I love ya!
Sed vero, spectatores amabilissimi fuistis! Vos amo! Vos amo!

A SIDESPLITTING LATIN TELEPHONE ANSWERING-MACHINE PRANK

First call:

This is the Vatican calling for the pope. We need a ruling on a venial sin.

Hoc est Vaticanum. Pontificem maximum filo vocamus. Nobis opus est arbitrio de peccato veniale.

Second call:

This is the College of Cardinals calling for the pope. We hope you can make it to the tailgate party next Saturday.

Hoc est Conlegium Cardinalium pontificem maximum filo vocans. Speramus te venturas esse ad convivium in tergis raedarum die Saturni proxima.

Third call:

This is the caretaker at Castel Gondolfo. Your Holiness, do you want me to prune these olive trees?

Hic est custo Castelli Gondolfi. Papa Sanctissime, visne ut illas oleas putem?

Fourth call:

Hi, this is the pope. Have there been any messages for me?

Ave, hic est pontifex maximus qui tibi filo dicit. Mihine nuntia ulla fuerunt?

A LATIN TONGUE TWISTER

How much wood would a woodchuck chuck if a woodchuck
   could chuck wood?
*Quantum materiae materietur marmota monax si marmota monax
   materiam possit materiari?*

Just as much wood as a woodchuck would if a woodchuck
   could chuck wood.
*Tantum materiae quam materietur marmota monax si marmota
   monax materiam possit materiari.*

THINGS TO SAY AT A TOGA PARTY

Are you wearing anything under that sheet?
Ullamne subuculam geris?

Toga! Toga! Toga!
Toga! Togae! Togam!

AN ALL-PURPOSE WEDDING TOAST

I'd like to propose a toast to the happy couple and their
   incompatibility: His *income*, and her *pat-ability!*
Ego coniugibus felicibus propino: Scin quam inter se diversitas sit?
   Is dives, ea versuta est!

AN ALL-PURPOSE LATIN AFTER-DINNER SPEECH

You probably all think I am going to say something weighty and memorable in Latin. Well, I'm not. What I'm going to do is read you my laundry list. Here it is. Three pairs of socks, five underwear, two shirts, no starch. There, that's it. You can applaud now. Have a nice day.

Vos omnes fortasse creditis me aliquid grave ac memorabile Latine dicturum esse. Re vera, illud facere non in animo habeo. Etenim perlegam vobis catalogum lavandorum. Hic incipit. Tibialium paria tria, subuncularum quinque, tunicae duae, nullum amylum. Sic, actum est. Mihi plaudere nunc potestis. Die dulci fruimini.

XVI.
INTERNATIONAL LATIN

Lingua Latina Foris

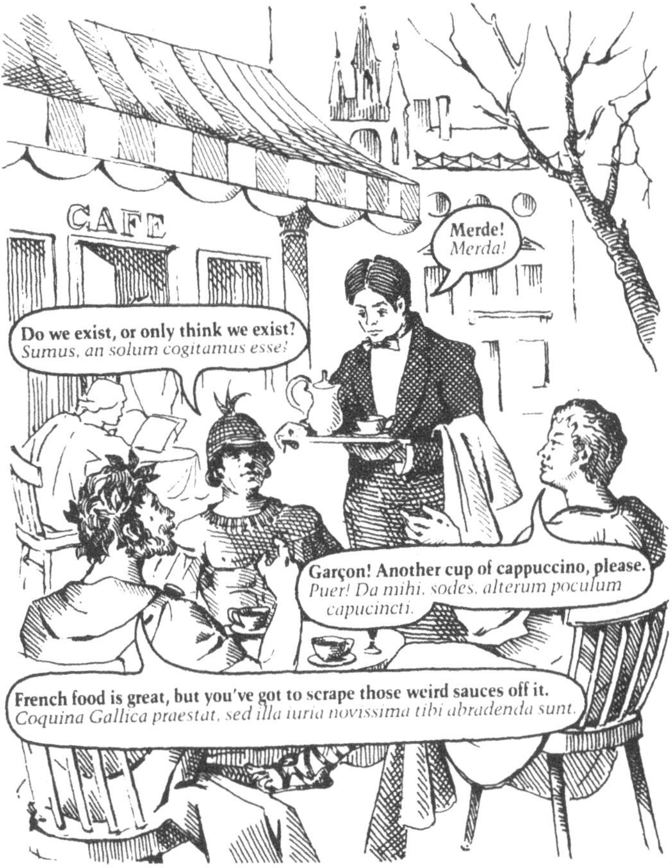

AT THE AIRPORT

How long will the flight be delayed?
Quanta mora volatui fiet?

What do you mean, you're overbooked?
Ain, supra modum sedes conductae sunt?

Is there a way to get there without going through Atlanta?
Potestne illuc pervenire Atlantum tamen praeteriens?

Do I get frequent flier miles for the walk between gates?
*Daturne praemium plurima milia passuum volandi mihi tantum
     spatium gresso inter portas?*

How about an upgrade?
Velisne me extollere ad cursum pretiosiorem?

Stand aside, plebeians! I am on imperial business!
Recedite, plebes! Gero rem imperialem!

ON AN AIRPLANE

Will this seat go back any further?
Haecine sedes potest ultro reclinari?

No, I don't want a red-hot towelette.
Minime! Nolo mantele candens.

Is *Pet Health* the only magazine you have?
Estne Valetudo Animalium Domesticorum *periodicus libellus solus quem ad manum habes?*

What is the movie on the flight?
Quis est cinematographia in hoc volatu?

And you expect me to pay for the headphones?
Et credisne me empturum esse conchas soniferas?

I'll have a Bloody Mary, please.
Velim sumere Mariam Sanguinariam, sis.

Could you get that baby to shut up?
Potesne compescere ululuatum istius infantis?

Don't you have anything besides Salisbury Steak and Chicken Cacciatore?
Nonne alium cibum habes praeter Bubulam Sorbiodunensem et Pullum Coctum Modo Venatoris?

Hey, you've been in there for twenty minutes.
Heia, viginti iam minutas in latrina ines.

Yeah, it was a great flight. Now where do I go to get branded and have my hooves dipped?
Sic, volatus praestat. Nunc quo vadam ut nota in me inuratur et ungulae medicamentis mergantur?

AT THE RENTAL-CAR COUNTER

I don't want a subcompact.
Nolo cisium exiguum.

I reserved a midsize.
Currum medium conduxi.

Does this insurance cover me if I get sideswiped by some
    bastard in a chariot with knives on its wheels?
Subveniatne mihi haec fides damni resarciendi interposita si deiciar
    a nescioquo furcifero agente currum falcatum?

THINGS TO SAY ON A CRUISE SHIP

I hate shuffleboard.
Ludum tabulaticum odi.

What time is lunch?
Quando prandimus?

Hey, Captain, why don't you open her up and see what this
    baby can do?
Agedum, Magister, habenas dans monstra quam velociter hic
    phaselus currere possit!

How do you say "Man overboard!" in English?
Quomodo dicitur Anglice "Vir in mare excidit!"?

Are we sinking?
Summergimurne?

Women, children, and Latin speakers first!
Feminae, infantes atque homines qui Latine loqui possint
    antecedant!

THINGS TO SAY ON THE ORIENT EXPRESS

Quick, pretend you know me!
Cito, simula me cognoscere!

See that man? He's a spy for the German tribes.
Videsne illum? Explorator Germanicus est.

I have the plans for the new multiple independently targeted,
boulder-hurling catapult. *Shhh!*
*Descriptiones habeo catapultae novae quae saxos multos separatim
et simul iaciant. St!*

If he gets his hands on them, it will be the end of the world
as we know it.
Si illas prehendat, sit finis terrae qualem cognovimus.

So, where are you headed?
Quo vadis?

THINGS TO SAY IN A SIDEWALK CAFE

How do we know whether we actually exist or only *think* we
exist?
*Quemadmodum possumus scire utrum vere simus an solum
sentiamus non esse?*

Can we ever truly distinguish art qua art from that which is
merely pleasing to the eye?
*Possumusne umquam vero artem ipsam secernere ab illis quae modo
oculis grata sint?*

Could I get another cup of this great cappuccino and one of
   those little chocolate pastries?
*Da mihi, sodes, alterum poculum huius capucincti suavissimi et
   unum e crustulis illis theobromaticis?*

YOU SOUND LESS LIKE A TOURIST WHEN YOU GAWK IN LATIN

Boy, if these old walls could talk!
Edepol, utinam hi parietes veteres dicere possint!

How much do you think a painting like that would set you
   back?
Quanto credis picturam illius notae tibi staturam?

If you sit on one of those chairs with a little rope across it, do
   you get a shock?
*Si quis in unam ex illis sedibus, quibus funiculus est impositus,
   adsidat, cadat quasi fulmine stratus?*

That's the biggest bed I've ever seen.
Ille lectus est quem maximum vidi.

How would you like to have a layout like this?
Nonne velis possidere latifundium similem huius?

You could put a satellite dish on that turret.
*Possis, si vellis, in illa turricula ponere lancem ad stellas mechanicas
   auscultandas.*

There's enough room here for an eighteen-hole golf course.
*Hic satis est spatium cursui ludi paganici Caledonii foraminum
   duodeviginti.*

But I bet the taxes and upkeep are murder.
Sed reor exactiones et impensas mortiferas esse.

I wonder where the gift shop is.
Scire velim ubi taberna munusculorum sit.

THINGS TO SAY AT THE VATICAN

Know where I can get a cup of coffee around here?
Scisne ubi pocillum coffeae in hoc vicinio possim comparare?

Is this the way to the Sistine Chapel?
Haecine via ducit ad Capellam Sextinam?

Is it all right to use a flash in here?
Licetne mihi hic fulgare uti?

Now *that's* a ceiling!
Ecce lacunar mirum!

Is this the only gift shop?
Haecine taberna munusculorum unica est?

Excuse me, can you recommend a good restaurant nearby?
*Ignosce mihi, potesne mihi recommendare popinam bonam
    vicinam?*

Where can I get a hat like that?
Ubi possum emere petasum similem isti?

XVII.
ESSENTIAL LATIN
Lingua Latina Necessaria

CHANCE ENCOUNTERS ARE LESS IN AWKWARD IN LATIN

Look what the cat dragged in!
Aspice quod felis attraxit!

Long time no see!
Tam diu minime visu!

Where have you been hiding yourself?
Ubi tere occultabas?

Let's not be strangers!
Non simus inter nos advenas!

See you later, alligator!
Vale, lacerte!

Don't do anything I wouldn't do!
Noli aliquid facere quod non faciam!

Jeepers, what a ying-yang!
Edepol, qualem praeputium!

AFFIRMATIONS ARE MORE AFFIRMATIVE IN LATIN

I'm not just whistling "Dixie"!
Non modo sibilo "Terram Dixonis!"

Does a bear shit in the woods?
Cacatne ursus in sylvis?

Does the pope speak Latin?
Loquiturne pontifex maximus Latine?

Word!
Verbum!

RATIONALIZATIONS ARE MORE RATIONAL IN LATIN

If I hadn't done it, someone else would have.
Si id non fecissem, aliquis id fecisset.

Everyone does it.
Sic faciunt omnes.

What they don't know won't kill them.
Quod nesciunt eos non interficiet.

So what's it to you, anyway?
Num curae est tibi?

A GOOD DEFENSE IS EVEN BETTER IN LATIN

I don't know what you're talking about.
Nescio de quo loqueris.

There's obviously been some sort of silly mistake.
Manifesto nescio quis lapsus stultus factus est.

You must be mad.
Vere furis.

Is this your idea of a joke?
Hocine tibi habeas iocum?

Can you actually prove any of that?
Potesne vere ullam partem probare?

That's my story, and I'm sticking to it.
Quae narravi, nullo modo negabo.

WIRETAPPERS DON'T KNOW LATIN

Whaddya say we bump him off?
Placetne tibi ut eum necemus?

Let's stick up the joint.
Locum despoliemus.

I got the stuff—you got the money?
Materiem habeo—habesne nummos?

Swell! Hey, you know what I'm gonna do? I'm gonna evade
all the income taxes on it!
*Bene! At scin quid faciam? Certum est mihi subterfugere omnia
vectigalia ei imposita!*

COMEBACKS ARE SNAPPIER IN LATIN

Says who?
Quis est qui inquit?

Is that a fact?
Vere dicis?

T.S.!
D.M.!

So's your old man!
Atque vetulus tuus!

PUT-DOWNS ARE MORE FINAL IN LATIN

Who rattled your cage?
Quis caveam tuam quassit?

Well, pardon me for living.
Vae, da mihi veniam vitae.

Get a life.
Fac ut vivas.

Be real.
Veritatem imitare.

Wake up and smell the coffee.
Expergiscere et coffeam olface.

TALK IS NEVER CHEAP IN LATIN

You're dead meat.
Caro putrida es.

You'll never work in this town again.
In hoc oppido nunquam postea operaberis.

You can run, but you can't hide.
Potes currere, sed te occulere non potes.

Guys like you are a dime a dozen.
Capita similia tui aestimantur unius assis.

I have jerks like you for breakfast.
Verveces tui similes pro ientaculo mihi appositi sunt.

Read it and weep.
Lege et lacrima.

Don't make me laugh.
Ne feceris ut rideam.

I'm shaking, I'm shaking.
Pavesco, pavesco.

TERMS OF NON-ENDEARMENT

Airhead
Caput vacans

Bimbo
Muliercula

Buttface
Vultus natiformis

Cheese dong
Praeputium turpe

Creep
Cimex

Dolt
Vervex

Doofus
Blennus

Dork
Caudex

Mouthbreather
Hiator

Numbnuts
Vir testibus torpidis

Sleazeball
Pila foeda

Space cadet
Tiro astromachus

Turboslut
Moecha mobilis

Wannabe
Simulator

SELF-ASSERTIVENESS IS SIMPLER IN LATIN

Hey, we're all in line here!
Heus, hic nos omnes in agmine sumus!

No cutting in!
Noli insere te in agmen!

No, excuse me, I believe I'm next.
Immo, ignosce mihi, ordinem credo vocare me.

You're from New York, aren't you?
Nonne de Neo-Eboracensis es?

THREATS CARRY MORE WEIGHT IN LATIN

Watch out—you might end up divided into three parts, like
   Gaul.
Cave ne—tamquam Gallia, tu ipse in tres partes dividaris.

People will soon be referring to you in the past pluperfect
   tense.
*Homines de te in tempore praeterito plus quam perfecto de te mox
   loquentur.*

If I were you, I wouldn't walk in front of any catapults.
Cave ne ante ullas catapultas ambules.

FIGHTING WORDS ARE SAFER IN LATIN

What did you call me?
Quid me appellavisti?

Yeah, I'm talking to you.
Te quidem adloquor.

You want me to repeat that?
Visne illud iterare?

A comedian, huh?
Ita vero, esne comoedus?

Oh yeah? Your mother!
Itane? Tua mater!

You want to make something of it?
Visne aliquid de illo facere?

You and whose army?
Tutene? Atque cuius exercitus?

Let's step outside.
Foras gradiamur.

Well, if you don't understand plain Latin, I'm not going to
dirty my hands on you.
Bene, cum Latine loqui nescias, nolo manus meas in te maculare.

OUR ANCIENT ROMAN LEGAL HERITAGE

You have a right to remain silent while you are tortured—or,
   if you prefer, you are free to scream your head off.
*Ius habes tacendi dum torqueris—vel, si mavis, tibi licet magnopere
   vociferari.*

You have a right to maintain your total ignorance of the
   preposterous trumped-up charges brought against you in
   secret.
*Ius habes asseverandi te scire nihil quidquam de criminibus
   praeposteris atque commenticiis clam contra te inlatis.*

You have a right to examine the entrails of the animal we cut
   up to find out whether you were guilty or really, really
   guilty.
*Ius habes inspiciendi exta pecudis quam persecuimus ut
   comperiremus utrum nocens an nocentissimus esses.*

You have a right to be confronted in the arena by a lion. If
   you cannot afford a lion, one will be provided for you.
*Ius habes obeundi leonem in harena. Si non potes conducere leonem
   conducere, praebemus.*

If the lion finds you inedible, you have a right to request an
   aisle or a bulkhead seat on the galley-oar to which you will
   be chained for the rest of your life.
*Si leo te non inveniat esculentum esse, ius habebis ab nauarcho
   poscendi sedem aut interiorem aut exteriorem sub remo ad quem
   vinctus deges reliquam vitam.*

LATIN: THE MOTHER OF ALL TONGUES

First we're going to cut it off, then we're going to kill it.
Primum id abscidemus, tum id occidemus.

He didn't move it, and now he's going to lose it.
Illud non movit, ergo illud perdet.

I came, I saw, I kicked ass.
Veni, vidi, nates calce concidi.

Bring 'em on!
In nosmet impetum faciant!

Make no mistake—we will find the weapons of mass
destruction.
Nolite falli—tela late mortifera inveniemus.

Mission accomplished!
Munus perfectum est!

XVIII.
POP-CULTURAL LATIN
Lingua Latina Popularis

ALL COMICS ARE CLASSIC COMICS IN LATIN

It's a bird! It's a plane! It's Superman!
Avis est! Aeronavis est! Supervir est!

Holy subjunctives, Batman!
Sanctos subiunctivos, Virvespertilio!

Oh no, Spidey's having an identity crisis!
Eheu, Araneus dubitat qui ipse sit!

The Hulk broke up with his girlfriend!
Moles familiaritatem sibi cum amica dirupit!

Shazam!
Hercule!

CARTOONS ARE, WELL, CARTOONIER IN LATIN

What's up, Doc?
Quid agis, Medice?

I'll get you, you wascally wabbit!
Te capiam, cunicule sceleste!

I tought I taw a puddy tat!
Credidi me felem vidisse!

Thuffering thuccotash!
Farrago fatigans!

Beep-beep!
Cornu sono!

Ah-bee, ah-bee, ah-bee, that's all, folks!
Abeo, abeo, abeo, actum est, comites!

THE GOLDEN AGE OF TV IS EVEN MORE GOLDEN IN LATIN

Just the facts, ma'am.
Dic mihi solum facta, domina.

Sorry about that, chief.
Illius me paenitat, dux.

You bet your bippy!
Tuis pugis pignore.

The devil made me do it!
Diabolus fecit, ut id facerem!

Kiss my grits!
Osculare pultem meam!

Beam me up, Scotty!
Me transmitte sursum, Caledoni!

If you fail, the secretary will disavow all knowledge of your
   activities.
*Si fallatis officium, quaestor infitias eat se quicquam scire de factis
   vestris.*

YOU'D HAVE BEEN ALLOWED TO LISTEN TO LATIN RADIO ALL NIGHT

What's behind that creaking door?
Quid pone illud ostium crepans situm est?

The Shadow knows.
Umbra scit.

Who was that masked man?
Quis fuit ille personatus?

Hi-ho, Silver, away!
Eeia, Argentei, eamus!

Good night, Mrs. Calabash, wherever you are.
Vale, era Curcurbita, ubicumque sis.

THE ALL-TIME TOP X

I Heard It Through the Grapevine
Hoc Fama Mihi, Cursum Sinuosum Secuta, Nuntiat

Itsy Bitsy Teeny Weenie Yellow Polka Dot Bikini
*Ceston atque Cingulum Parvissimos Minutissimos Natatorios
   Flavos Occelatos*

The 59th Street Bridge Song (Feelin' Groovy)
Cantus Pontis Viae Undesexagesimae (Laetans)

Stop in the Name of Love
Siste in Nomine Amoris

Shake, Rattle, and Roll
Treme, Strepe, et Volutare

These Boots Are Made for Walking
Caligae ad Ambulandum Factae Sunt

Be True to Your School
Fidelis Scholae Tuae Esto

You Can't Always Get What You Want
Non Potes Semper Capere Quod Aves

Diamonds on the Soles of Her Shoes
Sunt Adamantes in Solis Calceorum Suorum

Everybody's Got Something to Hide Except for Me and
My Monkey
Habent Abdenda Omnes Praeter Me ac Simiam Meam

WRITE YOUR OWN LATIN B-MOVIE SCRIPT

Huge flying discuses have landed in the Campus Martius!
Orbes immanes volantes in Campum Martium advenerunt!

It's horrible! These creatures have the head of a lizard and the
  body of a Helvetian!
*Horribile dictu! His animalibus biformibus sunt caput lacerti
  iunctum ad corpus Helvetii!*

Our weapons are useless against them!
Tela nostra nihil nobis prosunt in illos.

Send for the Greek thinker! Perhaps he can save us with his
  arcane arts!
Arcesse Palameden! Forsitan possit nos servare artibus suis abditis!

It's MMMMMMM to I, but it's our only chance—a flame-
  hurling catapult!
*Cum sit periculum tremendum, res tamen in aleam nobis danda
  est—ecce catapulta quae liquorem ardentem iacit!*

It's so crazy it might just work!
Tam insulsum est ut fortasse expediat.

Incredible! The Greek fire is melting them like wax!
Incredibile est! Ignis Graecus illos dissolvit quasi e cera facti sint!

Is it The End, or The Beginning of The End, or The End of
  The Beginning, or The Beginning . . . ?
Estne Finis, aut Initium Finis, aut Finis Initii, aut Initium . . . ?

THE SEVEN DWARVES GAIN MORE STATURE IN LATIN

Dopey
Fatuus

Doc
Medicullus

Grumpy
Severus

Happy
Beatus

Sleepy
Somniculosus

Bashful
Verecundus

Sneezy
Sternuens

NOSTALGIA IS MORE NOSTALGIC IN LATIN

Let's have a Tupperware party!
Habeamus convivium ad mercem emendam Tupperi!

Let's turn on the lava lamp!
Accendamus lucernam plenam massae ardentis!

Let's all wear mood rings!
Annulos qui animum ostendunt omnes gestemus!

Let's have a sock hop!
In tibialibus saltemus!

IMMORTAL HEADLINES FROM *THE CLASSICAL ENQUIRER*

PUER PATREM CAEDIT, MATREM SUAM IN MATRIMONIUM DUCIT
YOUTH KILLS HIS DAD, MARRIES OWN MOM

*CUM BELUA BARBARA IN LABYRINTHO NEFANDO PUGNAT: SEMIVIR, SEMIBOS
    CARNEM HUMANAM EDIT*
HE BATTLES WEIRD BEAST IN HELLISH MAZE: HALF-MAN, HALF-BULL
    DINED ON HUMAN FLESH

*REX DEMENS INFANTES FRATRIS SUI INTERFICIT COQUITQUE, TUM CENAM
    FOEDAM PARENTI HORRIFICATO APPONIT*
MAD KING SLAYS AND COOKS HIS BROTHER'S TOTS, THEN SERVES
    LOATHSOME DISH TO TYKES' HORRIFIED POP

THE ROMANS HAD CULTURE WARS, TOO

The only proper marriage is between a pagan man and a
    pagan woman. If we start letting deviant monotheistical
    Christians tie the knot, this empire will decline and fall,
    pronto.
*Iustum matrimonium tantum inter cultorem et cultricem deorum
    contrahi potest. Si incipamus sinere istos Christianos pravos,
    cultores dei quem unicum praedicant, nuptias inter se facere,
    imperium nostrum mox deficiens delabetur.*

If you want to take away my catapult, you are going to have
    to pry that big heavy rock from my cold, dead, somewhat
    bruised hands.
*Si velis mihi catapultam auferre, necesse tibi erit e manibus meis
    gelidis mortuis subtusis extorquere illud saxum grave.*

You can go ahead and teach geometry in the schools, but only as a theory, because it's just as likely that those strangely regular shapes are the sacred footprints of the god Apollo.

Te quidem licebit in scholis docere geometriam, dummodo pro theoria, quoniam tam veri simile est illas figura mirifice ordinatis vestigia sacra esse Apollonis.

BE YOUR OWN AD EXEC WITH LINGO FROM THE VIA MADISONIS

Let's run it up the flagpole and see if anybody salutes it!
Id in summum longurium quasi vexillum tollamus ut videamus utrum quis id salutet, necne!

Let's put it in the Colosseum and see if the lions will eat it!
Id in Colosseo ponamus ut videamus utrum leones id edant, necne!

Let's divide it into three parts and see if anybody conquers it!
Id in tres partes dividamus ut videamus utrum quis id vincat, necne!

Let's make it emperor and see if anybody assassinates it in the Forum!
Id imperatorum faciamus ut videamus utrum quis in Foro id interficiat, necne!

IMMORTAL TAGLINES ARE EVEN MORE CLASSIC IN LATIN

It takes a tough man to make a tender chicken.
Solus fortis et durus pullum tenerum parare potest.

Tastes great! Less filling!
Iucunde sapit! Minime implet!

I can't believe I ate the whole thing.
Non possum credere me totum edisse.

It's ugly, but it gets you there.
Deformis est, sed te illuc fert.

Where's the beef?
Ubi est bubula?

MORONIC TAG LINES ARE SLIGHTLY MORE BEARABLE IN LATIN

Please don't squeeze the Charmin!
Sis, noli Volvivoluptatem comprimere!

It's the quicker picker-upper
Tollit velocius.

I liked the shaver so much, I bought the company.
Tantum novaculum amabam, societam emi.

My wife—I think I'll keep her.
Uxor mea—Credo me eam semper retenturum.

Just do it.
Modo fac.

XIX.
CELEBRATIONAL LATIN
Lingua Latina Festiva

You know, we really ought to have turkey more often.
Opinor vere meleagridem gallopavonem nobis saepius edendum esse.

Is there a vomitorium in this house?
Adestne in hac domo vomitorium?

What actually is the difference between a yam and a sweet potato?
Quomodonam dioscorea et ipomoea inter se differunt?

THINGS TO SAY ON YOUR BIRTHDAY

Happy birthday to me!
Diem natalem felicem mihi!

For me? You shouldn't have!
Mihi? Opus non fuit!

I never would have guessed!
Nunquam coniectaverim!

It's just what I wanted!
Est admodum quod volui!

Where on earth did you find it?
Ubi gentium illud invenisti?

Do you happen to know offhand what their policy is on
    returns?
Scisne forte quid soleant agere cum res reductis?

THINGS TO SAY AT A BAR MITZVAH

This is delicious. What is it?
Iucunde sapit. Quid est?

May I have some more smoked salmon?
Da mihi, sis, plus salmonis fumosi?

THINGS TO SAY ON GROUNDHOG DAY

How do you know you have the right groundhog?
Ut scis te observare marmotam monacem ipsam?

What happens if he wanders out on a highway and gets run
   over by a truck? Do we get an ice age?
*Quid fiat si in viam erret et a vehiculo magno conculcetur? Saeclum
   glaciale?*

LATIN VALENTINES FOR ST. VALENTINE'S DAY

Roses are red, violets are blue,
   Gaul is divided into three parts,
   And so will my heart be if I ever lose you!
Rubore di tinxerunt rosas
   Caeruleo di tinxerunt violas
   Cor meum in partes tres dividatur si tu me umquam relinquas!

Roses are red, violets are blue,
I don't care if the Carthaginians keep Carthage,
So long as I always have you!
Rubore di tinxerunt rosas
Caeruleo di tinxerunt violas
*Ita Carthaginienses Carthaginem habere possint ut semper
   habeam meas delicias!*

THINGS TO SAY ON ST. PATRICK'S DAY

Erin, go bragh!
Hibernia in aeternum!

If I drink this funny-looking beer, will my pee turn green, too?
Si bibam hanc cerevesiam, quae speciem insolitam praebet, urinane mea eveniet quoque viridans?

May all your nouns and adjectives agree in gender and number . . .
Nomina omnia et nomina adiectiva tua in genere et numero congruant . . .

May you always use the subjunctive properly. . . .
Modo subiunctivo recte utaris. . . .

And may you never accidentally try out your Latin on a Jesuit.
Et casu Latine loqui cum sodali Societatis Jesu ne umquam coneris.

THINGS TO SAY AT EASTER

If he's the Easter Bunny, where does he get the eggs?
Si Cuniculus Paschalis sit, unde ova capiat?

Maybe they're really brought by the Easter Lizard or the Easter Snake.
Forsitan re ipsa Lacerta Paschalis vel Anguis Paschalis illa ferat.

HANDY MESSAGES FOR EVERYONE'S LEAST FAVORITE HOLIDAYS

Dear Mom:

 I know I never write, I know I never call,
 I'm really most contrite, but I've been very busy in Gaul.
 Happy Mother's Day.

Cara mater mea:

 Scio me tibi non umquam scribere, scio me tibi non filo dicere,
 Huius me valde paenitebat, sed mihi in Gallia opus erat.
 Felici die maternali fruere.

Dear Dad:

 I'm not too proud to pen it: You never got your due.
 That's why I've asked the Senate to name a salad for you.
 Happy Father's Day.

Care pater mi:

 Vere, id mihi scribendum est: Multum tibi debendum est.
 Igitur cogito Senatum rogare acetaria ex te rite appellare.
 Felici die paternali fruere.

THINGS TO SAY AT GRADUATION

Hey, this diploma is in English!
Vae! Hoc diploma Anglice scriptum est!

Gyp! Gyp! I want my money back!
Fraudem! Fraudem! Mea pecunia vobis redenda est!

THINGS TO SAY ON THE FOURTH OF JULY

Wow! Did you see that one?
Hercle! Illud vidistine?

Look! This one's going to be even bigger!
Aspice! Hoc etiam grandius erit!

Ooooooooo!
Uuuuuuuuu!

THINGS TO SAY ON HALLOWEEN

Trick or treat!
Dolus vel dulce!

Sorry, kids, all I have is olives and figs.
Mihe, paenitet, pueri, sed nihil aliud habeo nisi olivas et ficos.

What do you mean, "nice costume"? This is my best toga!
*Quid vis dicere, "vestitus theatralis suavis"? Haec est mea toga
    optima!*

That mask isn't very scary. Have you ever seen a Helvetian?
Larva illa non est formidolosior. Umquam vidisti Helvetium?

Do you know what a catapult is?
Novistine quid sit catapulta?

If you're thinking of putting toilet paper on my house, ask
   yourself if you can outrun a ninety-mile-an-hour rock.
Si in animis habeatis scidam latrinariam in domo mea ponere,
   vosmet rogate si possitis velocius currere quam saxum quod vadit
   cum celeritate nonaginta milia passuum per horam.

THINGS TO SAY AT THANKSGIVING

I'd like to help, but I only know how to cut up birds for
   purpose of augury.
Cum velim te iuvare, solum tamen scio aves secare ad augurandum.

What actually is the difference between a yam and a sweet
   potato?
Quomodonam dioscorea et ipomoea inter se differunt?

You know, we really ought to have turkey more often.
Opinor vere meleagridem gallopavonem nobis saepius edendum esse.

I'll have some more mashed potatoes and gravy.
Da mihi, amabo, plus solanorum tuberosorum tunsorum et iuris.

Oh boy, pumpkin pie!
Euax, crustum cucurbitae peponis!

Um, do you by any chance happen to have a vomitorium in
   this house?
En, habeasne forte in hac domo vomitorium?

THINGS TO SAY ON HANUKKAH

Happy Hanukkah!
Hanukka felicem vobis!

So enough already with the Latin-Schmatin. Let's eat.
Iam est satis superque linguae Latinae-Fatuinae. Edamus.

THINGS TO SAY AT CHRISTMAS

Bah! Humbug!
Phy! Fabulae!

Christmas has gotten too commercial.
Dies natalis Christi nimis mercatoria facta est.

I'll have some more of that eggnog.
Sumam plus oögalactos.

So, who do you like for the Super Bowl?
Bene, cui in Colosseo Maximo faves?

NEW YEAR'S RESOLUTIONS ARE LESS BINDING IN LATIN

This year I am definitely going to . . .
Hoc anno ego pro certo . . .

   go on a diet.
   dietam sequi incipiam.

get more exercise.
musculos saepius exercebo.

attend more cultural events.
adsidue bonis artibus studere.

make larger charitable contributions.
liberalius largiar.

be nicer to people.
benignius aliis me geram.

stop misusing the subjunctive.
abuti modo subiunctivo desinam.

XX.
LOCUTIO LINGUAE LATINAE PAUCIS VERBIS EXPLANATUR

A Brief Guide to Latin Pronunciation

VOWELS

a if long, as in "bl<u>ah</u>"; if short, as in "rub-<u>a</u>-dub"
e if long, as in "ol<u>e</u>"; if short as in "f<u>eh</u>"
i if long, as in " 'z<u>i</u>ne"; if short as in "z<u>i</u>t"
o if long, as in "d'<u>oh</u>"; if short as in "n<u>o</u>t"
u if long, as in "d<u>u</u>de"; if short as in "wass<u>up</u>"

There is really no simple way to tell if a vowel is long or short, but if the word is short—one syllable—treat the vowel as short. The last syllable of verb endings are almost always short. If *a*, *i*, *o*, or *u* come at the end of a word, they're long; if *e* comes at the end of a word, it's short. If a vowel is followed by two consonants, it's long. For other situations, *pronuntia utrolibet modo!* (wing it).

DIPHTHONGS

ae as in "T<u>hai</u>"
au as in "<u>ou</u>ch"
ei as in "h<u>ey</u>"
eu as in "<u>hey</u>, <u>you</u>"
oe as in "g<u>oy</u>"
ui as in "pt<u>ui</u>"

CONSONANTS

b, d, f, h, l, m, n, and **p** are the same as in English. So are **k** and **z**, which are rare in Latin anyway. *j*, *w*, and the consonant *y* don't exist in Latin.

c, ch always "k"
That's a KIGH-sahr salad you ordered. You want ANN-koh-veese with that?

g, gn always "<u>guh</u>"
The Romans were fighting the GUHR-mahns, not the JUR-mahns, and when they gave the signal to attack, it was a SIHG-nuhm (trumpet blast) not a SEE-nuhm (large bowl)

i always "<u>yuh</u>"
It's thanks to YOO-lih-uhss (not JOO-lee-yuss) that we celebrate the fourth of July instead of the fourth of Quinctil

r you can rrroll your r's even if they'rrre the last let-terrrr of a worrrrd

s always "sss"
The Roman fanss (not fanz) were animalss (not animalz)

t, th always "<u>teh</u>"
Teh-hey teh-rew teh-hings at eak ot-her during teh-he nah-tih-oh-nahl (not nashunal) ant-hem (not anthum)

v   always "w"
          The wolcano that waporized Pompeii was Weh-SOO-wee-uhss

There are no silent letters in Latin. Every vowel (unless it's part of a two-syllable diphthong) and every consonant is always pronounced fully and is often pronounced separately. There are also no actual Romans around to give you the stink-eye when you mess up.